THE DECADES OF TWENTIETH-CENTURY AMERICA

AMERICA IN THE 1990s

MARLENE TARG BRILL

Twenty-First Century Books · Minneapolis

Twenty-First Century Books
A division of Lerner Publishing Group, Inc.
241 First Avenue North
Minneapolis, MN 55401 U.S.A.

Website address: www.lernerbooks.com

Library of Congress Cataloging-in-Publication Data

Brill, Marlene Targ.
    America in the 1990s / by Marlene Targ Brill.
        p.   cm. — (The decades of twentieth–century America)
    Includes bibliographical references and index.
    ISBN 978–0–8225–7603–7 (lib. bdg. : alk. paper)
    1. United States—History—1969– —Juvenile literature. 2. United
States—Civilization—1970– —Juvenile literature. 3. Popular culture—
United States—History—20th century—Juvenile literature. 4. Nineteen
nineties—Juvenile literature. I. Title. II. Title: America in the nineteen
nineties.
    E881.B75 2010
    973.92—dc22   2009011628

Manufactured in the United States of America
1 2 3 4 5 6 – VI – 15 14 13 12 11 10

CONTENTS ★★★★★★★★★★★★★★★★★

Friends enjoy a video game on a PERSONAL HOME COMPUTER in 1983. In the 1990s, computerized technology would grow by leaps and bounds.

ENTERING THE DIGITAL AGE

I remember the advent of the nineties very clearly," wrote Steve Case, cofounder of America Online (AOL), a major Internet service. "It was a time of big ideas and events. . . ."

Many Americans shared Case's impression of the early 1990s. They entered the final decade of the twentieth century ready for major changes. Since 1981 Music Television (MTV) had been bringing new sounds, artists, and fashions into living rooms across the country. The generation raised during the 1980s was the first to grow up with music videos, VCRs, handheld music players, and video cameras. These young Americans were primed to embrace new technology once reserved for science fiction.

■ INVENTION REVOLUTION

Computers had existed in some form since the 1940s. But early versions were clunky pieces of equipment that filled entire rooms. Only universities, government agencies, and large businesses could afford the space and professional skills needed for computer technology. The creation of desktop personal computers in the 1980s introduced families to home computers. Further advances in software, hardware, and operating systems improved the function and compatibility of computers. By 1990 users could blend word processing with accounting spreadsheets and

5

graphics. They could also dial into nationwide phone networks (early online services) and access news or shop from their computers.

While new communication technology developed at lightning speed—as in cordless and cellular phones, handheld cassette players, and compact disc players—prices of original models fell. Consumers could afford to enter the next decade as part of the digital age, the name given to this period of rapid technological advances.

The study of human genetics also opened doors to exciting medical developments. Scientists explored new techniques to repair body parts and cure disease. Researchers investigated ways to stop the acquired immunodeficiency syndrome (AIDS) epidemic, a pressing challenge by the mid-1980s. Between medical and computer advances, Americans began the 1990s looking ahead with enthusiasm for new developments.

■ THE REAGAN YEARS

Government was changing too. When President Ronald Reagan left office in 1989, most Americans felt good about their country. Gone was frustration about the government's weakness in the Iranian Hostage Crisis, which had marked the beginning of the 1980s. Reagan's sunny, patriotic speeches revived the idea of the United States as the world leader.

Reagan was a popular president, but his economic policies hurt much of the population. Wealthy people prospered, but poverty increased and scandals were widespread in business and politics under his administration. Years of military buildup to compete against the Soviet Union (USSR, a union of fifteen republics including Russia) had drained national finances. The United States spent more than it collected, so it slipped deeper into debt. The U.S. government accumulated the highest national debt since the 1920s.

The administration didn't want to raise taxes on the wealthy to help lower the debt. Instead, Congress removed restrictions on corporations and transportation companies. Reagan believed that businesses would expand and prosper—and thus benefit the economy—without laws to regulate their growth. He called his top-down plan the trickle-down economy. This deregulation triggered a rush of corporate mergers and buyouts that continued into the 1990s.

RONALD REAGAN explains his tax reduction policy in a televised address in 1981. In reality, only wealthy people benefited from Reagan's tax policy. Criticism of Reagan's policies seemed to slide off his smooth image as if it were a Teflon-coated pan. Because of this, some called Reagan the Teflon president.

In the United States, deregulation and a high national debt allowed foreign nations to invest and get a foothold in U.S. industries. Before this, laws protecting U.S. businesses hindered takeovers and investment from foreign countries. After deregulation any company with enough money and clout could enter U.S. markets. At the same time, local companies looked overseas for cheaper goods. These combined forces launched the global economy—a worldwide exchange of goods and services.

Those who managed the companies prospered. During the 1980s, many young employees also profited from the businesses' wealth, earning high salaries. They became known as yuppies, or young urban professionals. Yuppies typically focused on hard work, material wealth, and social status. As a result of the consumerism of these Americans, the eighties was characterized as a decade of excess. Going into the nineties, however, many Americans had soured on showy buying binges.

Unlike the yuppies, middle- and lower-income families suffered from corporate restructuring. Managers cut jobs to make blended U.S. companies more profitable. By the 1990s, unemployment had risen among those who could least afford to be jobless. Long-term, high-paying positions were replaced by lower-paying jobs, many from new big-box stores such as Wal-Mart and Costco. These chain-owned stores hit many communities hard. Low big-box prices drew customers away from locally owned establishments. Many small businesses folded after chain stores opened at suburban malls. With fewer jobs to go around, and wages unable to keep up with inflation, the number of homeless families climbed nationally.

■ NEW LEADERSHIP, AT HOME AND ABROAD

The global economy was a driving force in U.S. interactions with the rest of the world. The international scene was shifting rapidly by 1990. The Reagan administration made great strides toward ending the Cold War (1945–1991), the name given to post–World War II tensions between the United States and the Soviet Union. Reagan held groundbreaking talks with Mikhail Gorbachev, the Soviet leader. The two sought to reduce arms and increase trade.

Gorbachev also created a new order of government that gave Soviet citizens more individual freedoms than under previous leaders. Strict Soviet Communism is a system of government ownership of business and government-controlled distribution of wealth. It had oppressively ruled modern-day Russia and much of Eastern Europe since the 1920s. Gorbachev's change in policies became known as glasnost, meaning "openness" in Russian.

Reagan's vice president, George Herbert Walker Bush, was elected president in 1988. Bush hesitated to introduce his own foreign policy changes until he saw how the world adjusted to the changing Soviet Union. "I keep hearing the critics saying we're not doing enough on Eastern Europe," Bush wrote in his diary. "The longer I'm in this job, the more I think prudence [caution] is a value and experience matters."

Under glasnost, the Soviet government loosened control of its people, beginning at home. Eventually other Soviet-dominated nations sought their own independence. A major breakthrough against Communist power came in November 1989 when Germans tore down the Berlin Wall, which split the city of Berlin in two. Since 1961 this concrete wall had spanned the 27-mile (43-kilometer) border between East and West Berlin and stood as a symbol of East Germany's grim Communist regime.

One by one, Eastern European nations overthrew their Soviet-backed administrations and rejected Communism. They demanded private ownership of

On June 12, 1987, President Ronald Reagan spoke at the Berlin Wall from the **BRANDENBURG GATE** in Berlin, West Germany. In his famous speech there, he addressed Soviet leader Mikhail Gorbachev, saying, "If you seek peace . . . for the Soviet Union and Eastern Europe . . . Mr. Gorbachev, tear down this wall!"

businesses, free speech, free elections, and the ability to protest and cross borders without fear of losing their lives. Such progress silenced Bush's critics, who wanted him to be more forceful with the Soviets.

Bush took more forceful action on another foreign policy front. On December 20, 1989, Bush ordered twelve thousand U.S. soldiers to Panama, a Central American nation, to join another twelve thousand soldiers stationed there. His goal was to arrest Panama's dictator, General Manuel Noriega, for drug trafficking. President Bush also wanted to keep Noriega from interfering with the Panama Canal, the vital shipping route that connects the Atlantic and Pacific Oceans. (However, critics later charged that the real reason for going after Noriega was to stop him from revealing damaging Central Intelligence Agency (CIA) evidence against Bush, a former CIA director.)

After four days of fighting, the invasion ended with twenty-three U.S. soldiers and about five hundred Panamanians dead. On January 5, 1990, Noriega surrendered to U.S. authorities. The military defeat provided Bush with a quick victory that raised his star power with the American public. But this was not the Bush some had expected. In his inauguration speech, Bush had talked about making "kinder the face of the nation and gentler the face of the world," a direction he followed with the Soviets but not in Panama. Citizens wondered which Bush they would see in the future.

President George H. W. Bush SIGNS THE AMERICANS WITH
DISABILITIES ACT on the White House lawn in July 1990.

CHAPTER ONE
KINDER **NATION:**
MORE DIFFICULT WORLD

As the final decade of the twentieth century began, Americans were watching the world transform. They hailed the recent fall of Communism in Eastern European countries. But they were also keeping an eye on terrorism and conflicts new and old around the globe.

President Bush did not lose focus on domestic issues. In 1990 he moved toward the kinder nation he had promised, signing into law the most far-reaching bill against discrimination since the Civil Rights Act of 1964. The Americans with Disabilities Act guaranteed equal access for anyone with a disability to jobs, public places, transportation, state and local government services, and communication devices such as telecommunications devices for the deaf (TDDs) or voice-activated computers. One aim of the bill was to raise the employment level among disabled citizens, allowing more to support themselves without government help. But new mandates for accessible elevators, wheelchair ramps, or lifts also ensured more physical freedom. The law was hailed as a new declaration of independence for all Americans.

■ BROCCOLI BAN

President Bush drew national attention over a different kind of domestic issue by announcing his dislike of green vegetables, particularly broccoli. He declared, "I do not like broccoli. And I haven't liked it since I was a little kid and my mother made me eat it, and I'm President of the United States. And I'm not going to eat any more broccoli."

As a result, broccoli was banned from menus in the White House and on Air Force One, the presidential plane. The ban created an uproar with broccoli growers. They sent tons of broccoli to the White House in protest. Bush refused to reconsider. But the broccoli never went to waste. Aides distributed the banned green substance to food banks in the Washington, D.C., area.

■ THE PERSIAN GULF WAR

Persisting troubles halfway around the globe dogged the Bush administration. For decades, warring countries in the Middle East made the region a tinderbox. Tensions lingered between Iraq and Iran, which had fought a long war in the 1980s. The United States had secretly supplied arms or information to both sides but did not openly take part in the war until 1987, following attacks on U.S. vessels that were patrolling in the Persian Gulf. The administration determined Iran the greater threat and backed Iraq's leader Saddam Hussein by sending advanced weapons to support Iraq's military.

The Iran-Iraq War (1980–1988) ended in a cease-fire without a peace agreement. The long conflict left Iraq a scarred nation with a depleted economy. Saddam Hussein had directed all the nation's money into building a million-person army and developing chemical weapons capable of causing massive destruction.

President Bush and many Middle Eastern leaders thought Saddam Hussein was unstable. His dictatorship was ruthless. He had ordered the killing of entire communities of Kurdish citizens (members of an ethnic minority) in northern Iraq. Following the war, he was in debt and in control of a large army with modern weapons. Foreign leaders viewed him as a threat—a concern that proved correct.

On August 2, 1990, Iraqi tanks crossed the border into neighboring Kuwait. Saddam Hussein was determined to capture and take control of the small, oil-rich nation. Twenty-four hours later, Iraqi troops lined the Iraqi–Saudi Arabian border as well. A shudder of fear went through the international community. If Iraqi troops successfully moved into Saudi Arabia, Iraq would control 40 percent of the world's oil fields. This would allow Iraq to greatly influence the supply and pricing of oil. Unlike Saudi Arabia, Iraq was not friendly toward the United States and other Western nations. That much economic power in Saddam Hussein's hands could threaten many countries that depended upon foreign oil.

President Bush ordered thousands of U.S. troops into Saudi Arabia to protect its border. He contacted allies in the United Nations (UN), the international peacekeeping group, to agree on a plan of action. Bush gathered the support of thirty nations to block the Iraqi military, should force be necessary. "I have warned Saddam Hussein that any terrorist act against us or our allies will be his responsibility," the president wrote to King Hussein bin Talal of Jordan.

The UN gave Iraq until midnight on January 16, 1991, to remove troops from Kuwait. After Iraq refused to withdraw, U.S.-led forces began Operation Desert Storm. They launched air attacks targeting Iraq's communication, electric, water, and sewage systems, as well as military factories and camps. The U.S. military took orders from General Norman Schwarzkopf and General Colin Powell, the chairman of the Joint Chiefs of Staff.

Within thirty-eight days after the air strike began, the assault had destroyed or disabled most Iraqi military targets and cut Iraq's supply routes by 90 percent. The United States then led two hundred thousand ground troops against Iraqis in Kuwait. Fighting lasted one hundred hours before Bush called a cease-fire. The attack swiftly defeated Saddam Hussein's forces and pushed them back into Iraq.

A U.S. military aircraft flies over burning oil fields in Kuwait during **OPERATION DESERT STORM** in 1991. The retreating Iraqi forces set fire to Kuwait's oil fields as a tactic to waste that country's valuable resource. The fires caused international forces to divert time and resources away from the attack on Iraq in order to stop the blaze.

President Bush stopped short of an Iraq takeover. Secretary of State James Baker and other Bush administrators believed that removing Saddam Hussein would destabilize the entire Middle East. Hussein was a member of the Sunni Islamic sect, the largest branch of Islam but a minority branch in Iraq. He ruled with an iron hand to suppress non-Sunni religions and sects in Iraq. The Bush team determined that without Saddam, religious wars between Shiite and Sunni Islamic sects would erupt in Iraq. Similar religious battles could spill into neighboring Middle Eastern countries and cause widespread chaos. Members of the United Nations agreed. But they monitored Saddam Hussein to ensure that he destroyed his powerful weapons.

The Persian Gulf War was an efficient conflict. Battles were swift, calculated for the fewest casualties, and effective. The administration reported 148 allied soldiers dead and 458 wounded, but more than 200,000 Iraqis died. President Bush was hailed for his foreign diplomacy, having coordinated the support of so many nations. The successes in Panama and Kuwait portrayed Bush as a decisive leader. Critics, however, saw Bush as an imperialist, extending U.S. control in the world. They charged that the administration had gotten involved because of its own economic interest in the Middle East and Latin America. Nonetheless, Bush's job approval rating following the war reached 91 percent, the highest rating recorded for any president until that time.

■ CLARENCE THOMAS AND THE MEDIA CIRCUS

Bush ran into controversy with his nomination of Clarence Thomas to the Supreme Court. Thomas would replace retiring justice Thurgood Marshall, a civil rights champion and the first African American Supreme Court justice. Thomas's confirmation hearings were broadcast on several television news channels. But coverage of one Senate Judiciary Committee interview of Thomas on October 11, 1991, drew uncommon national attention.

The committee had already heard the usual appeals for and against Thomas. Some critics outside the hearing believed the president chose Thomas merely because he was African American and very conservative. They viewed Thomas as an average judge unworthy of the nation's highest court. The fifteen-member American Bar Association reviewing panel had rated him as "qualified," not "well qualified."

PROFESSOR ANITA HILL testified in the Clarence Thomas hearings. Hill brought damaging charges against Thomas in the 1991 Senate confirmation hearings for his appointment to the U.S. Supreme Court.

One critic was a woman who had worked for Thomas in two government agencies during the Reagan administration. Professor Anita Hill testified that Thomas repeatedly sexually harassed her, behavior unworthy of a Supreme Court justice. Thomas denied Hill's charges. Under the glare of television cameras, the all-male Senate committee asked Hill and Thomas detailed personal questions. Many viewers felt that Hill was treated especially roughly in the ordeal. They sensed that her accusations and testimony were not taken seriously enough. Viewers took sides and debated from their living rooms.

In the end, the Senate narrowly approved Thomas with a vote of 52–48. But a feeling of distaste remained after the entire televised process was over. As reporter Peter Jennings wrote, "There was among people on all sides the uncomfortable feeling of having just been party to an ugly public spectacle of extraordinary insensitivity, if not a 'high-tech lynching' [as Thomas had charged] then at the very least a 'high-tech humiliation' of two people whose murky relationship had been picked apart by a bumbling Senate panel."

■ ECONOMY WOES

The U.S. economy, hurting from the increased national debt and ineffective trickle-down policies of the eighties, had become a pressing issue for the Bush administration. In 1990 and 1991, the United States experienced severe job losses. Businesses were failing at a record rate. Both conditions meant less federal income from taxes to run the government. The nation also faced huge debts from the cost of the Persian Gulf War.

When nominated as Republican candidate for president, Bush had promised: "The Congress will push me to raise taxes and I'll say no, and they'll push, and I'll say no, and they'll push again. And I'll say to them, 'Read My Lips: No New Taxes.'" But with the growing deficit (the difference between the amount of money the government has in the treasury to pay for its programs and the larger amount that it spends), Bush saw that the government needed money.

Republicans and Democrats disagreed on the best course of action. Bush decided to back down on his campaign promise to voters. He announced: "It is clear to me that both the size of the deficit problem and the need for a package that can be enacted" called for several remedies, including "tax revenue increases." He admitted that meant possibly raising taxes in various ways. Critics charged that Bush's economic program was too little, too late. In addition, many voters felt betrayed by his tax plan and his inability to improve the economy. By early 1992, Bush's approval rating fell to only 43 percent.

■ THE MAN FROM HOPE

Candidates for the upcoming 1992 presidential election jumped on the struggling economy as a hot campaign issue. Democrats chose forty-six-year-old William (Bill) Jefferson Clinton, a five-term Arkansas governor, as their candidate for president. Clinton was a fast-track whiz kid who had taught law classes straight out of law school. He was Arkansas attorney general at the age of thirty and became the nation's youngest governor at the age of thirty-two. As governor he focused on improving education and boosting the Arkansas economy. Other governors had once named him "the nation's most effective governor."

Clinton, a warm, easygoing speaker, emphasized that he was a man of the people, unlike the wealthy Bush. Clinton was born in Hope, Arkansas, and raised in Hot Springs, Arkansas, by his mother and stepfather, an alcoholic who sometimes abused his wife. Clinton had financed college with scholarships and loans. He could feel the struggle and pain of others, he often said, because he had experienced those feelings during his upbringing.

GOVERNOR BILL CLINTON charmed audiences on the presidential campaign trail. He even played his saxophone for the audience of *The Arsenio Hall Show* in June 1992.

Clinton participated in a question-and-answer session on MTV to win the support of younger voters. His presentation excited MTV viewers. One reporter commented that Clinton was "the best politician I've ever seen in my life.... There's nobody who can work a crowd like he can ... and it's genuine when he's campaigning."

Other reporters dubbed Clinton "Slick Willy." He sidestepped tough questions about having avoided the army draft in 1969 because of his opposition to the Vietnam War (1957–1975). He smoothed over talk about his affairs with women. When asked about smoking marijuana, he claimed: "I experimented with marijuana a time or two, and I didn't like it. I didn't inhale it, and never tried it again." This denial of having inhaled dogged him as the butt of jokes.

Clinton positioned himself as a new kind of leader. He was from a middle-class family and was part of the baby boom generation, born between 1946 and 1964, in contrast with older, wealthy politicians such as President Bush. Clinton campaigned as an agent of change with middle-of-the-road views. The saxophone-playing, fast-food-eating governor called himself the Man from Hope, reflecting his birthplace and election theme.

■ THE PEROT EFFECT

Another candidate in the 1992 election, wealthy computer software businessman H. Ross Perot, ran as an independent. Perot was a self-made success story from Texas who built his company, Electronic Data Systems, into a billion-dollar business. His biggest clients included government agencies and big corporations. Yet he maintained a distrust of government and large organizations. Perot entered the campaign because he believed that his hard-driving business skills would solve the nation's economic problems.

Many people liked Perot's straightforward, folksy messages. But he abruptly dropped out of the race in mid-July, later claiming the Bush team planned to interfere with his daughter's wedding. One month before the November election, however, supporters urged him to reenter the race. Perot agreed, and his campaign caught fire. To get his message out, he spent $60 million of his personal fortune on television ads about how he would fix the economy.

President Bush's campaign claimed that his two opponents were too inexperienced to run a nation. Bush dismissed Clinton and his vice-presidential running mate, Al Gore, as "bozos." Bush singled out Gore as "ozone man" because Gore spoke out about the thinning ozone layer, which protects Earth from harmful sun rays. As for Perot, Bush seemed sure that people saw the short, feisty man as a "weirdo" with his big ears, high-pitched twang, and pushy style.

The public didn't buy Bush's assessments, and his poll ratings slipped. In the final months before the election, Bush campaign managers stepped up their smears on his opponents, leaking untrue or exaggerated information. While Bush touted his success in the Persian Gulf War, he attacked his opponents on character issues.

Voters disapproved of Bush's negative tone and believed he was out of touch with average citizens whose incomes were suffering. Clinton's team focused on what they saw as the nation's most pressing issue—the economy. James Carville, Clinton's campaign manager, kept a sign posted in the Clinton headquarters that read: "It's the economy, stupid!" In addition, the Clinton campaign embraced other everyday concerns such as education and health care.

> **" To renew America, we must be bold. . . . We must invest more in our own people, in their jobs, and in their future, and at the same time cut our massive debt. And we must do so in a world in which we must compete for every opportunity."**

—President Clinton, in his 1993 inaugural address

In the end, the public voted for change by electing the Man from Hope. Although not an overwhelming victory, Clinton won with 43 percent of the popular vote to Bush's 38 percent. At the age of forty-six, Bill Clinton became the nation's forty-second president. For a third-party candidate, Perot had received a respectable 19 percent. Bush claimed that "in the final analysis, Perot cost me the election."

The 1992 election also brought a record number of women to the House of Representatives and the Senate. Reporters dubbed these election successes the Year of the Woman. Some of the success was attributed to the effect of the Clarence Thomas–Anita Hill hearings. Those who felt Hill had endured unfair treatment in the hearings were determined to increase women's power in politics.

President Clinton entered office with an ambitious program for making life better for all Americans. However, he received no honeymoon period from Republicans or the media. Throughout his years in office, he attracted charges and criticism.

On March 12, 1993, President Bill Clinton *(left)* looks on as **JANET RENO** takes the oath of office to become the nation's first woman U.S. attorney general.

Several presidents are remembered for highlighting public service as an American value. In 1961 President John F. Kennedy established the Peace Corps, a government program that sends U.S. volunteers overseas to improve living conditions in developing areas. George H. W. Bush described the country's charitable organizations as "a thousand points of light." And in 1993, Bill Clinton created AmeriCorps, the largest government-sponsored effort to establish community programs within the United States.

This network of national service programs helps communities with education, health, public safety, and the environment. Based on the Peace Corps program, the AmeriCorps program trains workers to help change conditions in poor areas of the United States. Volunteers receive an allowance to pay for room and board, and after completing service, an education award to help pay for college or pay off student loans.

The first class of twenty thousand volunteers served in more than one thousand neighborhoods. At their 1994 swearing-in ceremony, President Clinton praised the graduates. "Service is a spark to rekindle the spirit of democracy in an age of uncertainty," he said. "When it is all said and done, it comes down to three simple questions: What is right? What is wrong? And what are we going to do about it? Today you are doing what is right—turning your words into deeds."

■ "DON'T ASK, DON'T TELL"

Clinton found himself in the middle of a controversial policy battle soon after taking office. His campaign had promised to allow gays and lesbians to serve openly in the military. Previously, anyone in the armed forces whose homosexuality became public received immediate discharge.

The president's intent to change that discriminatory policy was met with strong protests from Congress and military leaders. Nine days into his presidency, Clinton compromised on a "don't ask, don't tell" policy. As long as someone kept their sexual preference hidden, they could keep their uniform. The new policy aimed to end "witch hunts"—investigations into individuals' sexuality—and antigay harassment. Unlike earlier policies, it allowed homosexuals to serve in any capacity, including national security positions. If openly proclaiming their same-sex preference, however, soldiers still received the boot.

On February 5, 1993, Clinton signed the **FAMILY AND MEDICAL LEAVE ACT (FMLA)** in the White House Rose Garden.

The military establishment seemed pleased with the policy. Others believed it would continue long-standing abuse against homosexuals. Retired Republican senator Barry Goldwater of Arizona argued, "You don't need to be straight to fight and die for your country. You just need to shoot straight. That compromise doesn't deal with the issue—it tries to hide it."

■ FAMILY MATTERS

Clinton pledged to make working families a priority. Within a month after taking office, President Clinton fulfilled this campaign promise by signing the Family and Medical Leave Act. Under this law, workers could request up to twelve weeks of unpaid leave for family medical emergencies. For the first time, people with a new baby or sick child or parent could stay home without fear of losing their job.

Republican critics feared the bill would cost businesses too much. But Clinton noted that more parents were in the workforce than ever. He reasoned, "People who are worried about their infants or their sick parents are less productive than those who go to work knowing they've done right by their families."

■ GUN CONTROL

Crime was a hot issue during the early 1990s. Robberies and violent attacks increased at alarming rates. Reports indicated that two-thirds of murders in the United States were committed with guns.

Armed with these findings, President Clinton adopted an anticrime bill that included a ban on assault rifles and limits on access to guns. The bill required that gun buyers wait five days before acquiring handguns. After passing background checks, they could buy their guns. The bill was known as the Brady Act, after Ronald Reagan's press secretary, James Brady. Brady was disabled in the 1980s after being shot by a man attempting to kill President Reagan. The shooter had easily purchased a gun despite his history of mental illness.

At first President Clinton had difficulty getting the bill passed. Gun ownership groups, especially the National Rifle Association, lobbied against it. After ten days of bargaining, the Brady Act of 1993 passed in both houses of Congress. Observers credited Clinton's political arm-twisting with the victory.

The following year, Clinton's anticrime success continued with the approval of his Violent Crime Control and Law Enforcement Act of 1994, known simply as the Crime Bill. This measure designated enough federal money to hire one hundred thousand additional police and to fund crime-prevention education.

■ HEALTH-CARE REFORM

The Clinton administration's attempt to overhaul U.S. health care was one of its roughest battles. Health-care costs had been rising rapidly. Between 1980 and 1992, overall medical bills had tripled. The cost of hospital stays alone had risen almost 1,000 percent since 1950. Health insurance remained out of reach for about 39 million Americans. Canada, Australia, and some European nations offered national health-care programs for all citizens. Clinton wanted a similar program in the United States.

To head the health-care task force, the president chose his wife, Hillary Rodham Clinton. She was interested in doing much more as First Lady than being hostess at government functions.

In 1993 **HILLARY RODHAM CLINTON** presented the administration's plan to reform health care. Critics argued that Hillary wasn't elected—her husband was. President Clinton and supporters countered that they saw Hillary as the bonus of electing him—"two for the price of one."

Dartmouth-Hitchcock Medical Center

First Lady Hillary Rodham Clinton came to the White House with strong credentials. Raised in Park Ridge, Illinois, she excelled at Wellesley College and received her law degree from Yale Law School. After law school, she taught at the University of Arkansas Law School and worked as a lawyer. Once her husband became governor, she balanced her career with raising their daughter, Chelsea. She did public service to benefit Arkansas children and families. She actively campaigned for her husband's bid for president.

Hillary Clinton became the first presidential wife to have an office in the West Wing of the White House. As First Lady, she often consulted on policy decisions or took part in White House staff meetings. She accompanied Bill on many overseas trips and spoke out forcefully for women's rights worldwide. Her leadership on health-care reform was a landmark role for a First Lady. However, her nontraditional role sometimes created a stir.

During a campaign interview in 1993, when asked about continuing to work as a lawyer after her husband became governor, Clinton said, "I could have stayed home and baked cookies" but chose to use her talents elsewhere. Critics accused Clinton of putting down homemakers. She denied that she meant that and said her chocolate chip cookies compared well with anyone's recipe.

Family Circle magazine took her challenge. The magazine pitted her talents against then-First Lady Barbara Bush's by printing each of their chocolate chip cookie recipes. Readers voted for their favorite recipe. In the end, Clinton's recipe won over Bush's by 52 percent.

To some, the cookie war was a reminder of women's continued struggle for equal footing with men in U.S. society. Traditional views of women's roles were still pervasive. Hillary Clinton hoped to break that tradition.

23

However, some conservative men and women weren't comfortable with Hillary's active role in White House matters. But Clinton praised her talents, noting, "She's better at organizing people from a complex beginning to a certain end than anybody I've ever worked with in my life."

Clinton introduced his proposal in September 1993. But it never had a chance in Congress. Its overall aim—to provide health care for those not insured by an employer and to improve the quality of care for all—was overshadowed by the confusing details of the plan. Even Clinton insiders found it too complicated.

The strongest opposition came from drug makers and insurance companies that would lose profits if government took over health care. Companies ran misleading ads to block public support of the program. They played to fears of government mandates and inefficient bureaucracy. Some Republicans argued against the plan as "big government." Most people, left to sort through the flood of information, showed little confidence in the reform program.

After industry representatives lobbied Congress, Republican senators filibustered (extended debate to block a vote). Without enough support in Congress to override the filibuster, the health-care reform program died within a year.

■ SHOOTOUT AT WACO

The nineties saw a rise of extremist groups. These organizations were often critical of modern society and distrusted the government. In 1993 federal authorities clashed with one such group in Waco, Texas. The Branch Davidians of Waco were part of a Christian extremist religious sect. All members lived in a commune. The leader of the Waco Davidians claimed God had chosen him as a prophet and renamed him David Koresh. Koresh used his power to force sex on female Davidian members, including girls. He also used strict discipline that included beatings for children and timeouts in sewage pits for all members.

The Bureau of Alcohol, Tobacco and Firearms (BATF) had been investigating rumors that Davidians stockpiled illegal weapons and abused children. On February 28, 1993, the BATF raided the commune looking for weapons. They faced a hailstorm of bullets from the main building. The violent encounter left four BATF agents and several Davidians dead.

The Federal Bureau of Investigation (FBI) was then ordered to the scene. Federal agents circled the compound. For fifty-one days, agents kept up a twenty-four-hour assault of searchlights, buzzing helicopters, and blasting music to force the Davidians to surrender. In that time, twenty-one children and a number of adults were released from the commune, but many more remained.

Attorney General Janet Reno had command of the FBI. She and the president approved an attack to end the standoff. In the clash and fire that followed, eighty Davidians died, including Koresh and at least seventeen children.

Investigations into the fire indicated that a mass suicide attempt was to

On April 19, 1993, after a fifty-one-day siege by the FBI, flames destroyed the **BRANCH DAVIDIAN COMPOUND IN WACO, TEXAS.** David Koresh and many of his followers died inside.

blame for the loss of life. But some believed that dry conditions, agent gunfire, and gas might have ignited the fire. Either way, public response to the incident was a blow to Reno and Clinton. According to one report, "By 1999, a majority of the public believed that the FBI had murdered innocent people at Waco."

RISING SCANDAL

By 1994 Clinton's star had dulled for many citizens. Since before the 1992 election, Clinton had been ducking questions of sexual harassment. Paula Jones, who had worked for the state of Arkansas when Clinton was governor, accused him of sexual harassment in 1991. The administration rejected her accusations, and the following lawsuit was eventually dismissed.

The Clintons also faced questions about their real estate investments. The Whitewater Development Corporation, a failed real estate venture in Arkansas, was suspected of corruption. In August 1994, independent counsel Kenneth Starr took over an investigation of the Clintons' role in Whitewater. The investigation would drag on through the end of the decade.

Though the economy was slowly improving, political battles between the president and Congress overshadowed the progress. At midterm elections in 1994, only 39 percent of the 193 million eligible citizens voted, tossing out some longtime representatives in favor of change. Not one Republican congressional representative already in office suffered defeat. As a result, Republicans gained fifty-four seats in the House of Representatives and eight in the Senate to control both houses of Congress for the first time in forty years. The power shift occurred in state government as well.

NEWT GINGRICH, newly elected Republican speaker of the U.S. House of Representatives, raises his right hand during a swearing-in ceremony before Congress on January 4, 1995.

CHAPTER TWO

ROUGH TIMES:
POLITICS AND CURRENT EVENTS OF THE 1990s

Many credited Georgia representative Newt Gingrich with the Republican sweep in the 1994 elections. Gingrich had been working for years to put the Republican Party back in control of Congress. In the early 1990s, Gingrich launched a series of attacks against Democrats and the president. He mocked Hillary Clinton's failed health-care policy by dubbing it "Hillarycare." He pounded President Clinton for waffling on major issues and for personal misconduct. In 1995 these efforts were rewarded when fellow Republicans elected Gingrich Speaker of the House. He was also considered a frontrunner for the Republican nomination in the 1996 presidential election.

CONTRACT WITH AMERICA

Gingrich wanted to reform the U.S. government with a Republican revolution. He proposed an ambitious program called the Contract with America. His ten-point conservative agenda was designed to reshape the balance between federal and state governments. The points included balancing the budget, increasing the military, building prisons, and limiting welfare. The list appealed to the growing "religious right." This tight group of Christian conservatives, led by the Reverend Jerry Falwell, called themselves the Moral Majority. They had been an increasing influence in politics since 1980.

27

The Republican win in Congress and local elections signaled a huge shift in government direction. "From [President] Franklin Roosevelt onward, Americans came to accept the federal government as the solution to problems, a vast parental presence," wrote *Time* magazine's Lance Morrow. "Newt Gingrich wants to reverse the physics, make American government truly centrifugal [acting away from the center], with power flowing out of Washington . . . to the states."

Within one hundred days of becoming Speaker of the House, Gingrich pushed through twenty-six bills related to his Contract with America. However, just four became law. The president vetoed some, while Congress derailed others. Gingrich often lacked support from Democrats as well as from Republicans. Many bristled at his apparent ambition to become the party's star. Without a sense of crisis, few voters found enough interest to press for much of the Contract with America agenda.

By late 1995, polls showed disapproval of Gingrich and his promised revolution. But his leadership had left its mark by setting a more partisan tone in Washington, separating lawmakers by political party and ideology. As Speaker of the House, Gingrich pressed for legislation and investigations that deeply divided Congress. Compromise became more difficult than in the past. "I remember the sharp change . . . as if a hurricane had blown in," recalled economist Robert Reich, Secretary of Labor at the time.

■ BATTLE LINES CHANGE

The Contract with America helped focus the president's next issues. Clinton took the fire out of Republican assaults by embracing select Contract with America ideas. Against Democratic wishes, he led the call to overhaul the welfare system and balance the budget—two key Contract with America issues. He called for changes in Social Security, the nation's program of financial support for retired Americans and people with disabilities.

By November 1995, Clinton had recovered some of his political footing. He took a huge gamble and refused to back down in a battle with Republicans over the budget. The two sides debated tax breaks for the wealthy, a timeline for balancing the budget, and government aid programs. As the budget year closed without agreement, the president shut down the U.S. government. The shutdown made

The director of the Centers for Disease Control and Prevention—Dr. David Satcher—announces to reporters that the department will be severely scaling back operations due to the **1995 GOVERNMENT SHUTDOWN**.

headlines, and public opinion favored President Clinton. Many people had tired of partisan bickering. Finally, Congress compromised and approved a budget.

■ WELFARE REFORM

In 1996 Clinton yielded to Republicans in Congress on the details of welfare reform. Welfare programs assist those in poverty through financial help and support in finding employment. Conservatives objected to the cost of welfare and felt too many people in poverty were relying on the state instead of working. The Republicans' legislation restricted welfare aid more than Clinton's proposed reform would have. But under pressure to deliver on a campaign promise, Clinton agreed to sign the reform bill.

The resulting Personal Responsibility and Work Opportunity Reconciliation Act of 1996 limited welfare payments to five years. Money went only to families with a child or a pregnant woman. The U.S. government gave money to states in block grants. That meant state lawmakers distributed funds for programs as they saw fit. This system resulted in uneven assistance to the poor. The law did lower the numbers of welfare recipients and children in poverty. But some social service advocates criticized the bill—and Clinton—for leaving many poor families without a safety net.

■ THE 1996 ELECTION

President Clinton's fortunes had changed by the beginning of his reelection campaign in early 1996. His policies had improved the economy significantly, and excitement about the Republican Contract with America had died down. With Gingrich's light dimming, Republicans chose Kansas senator Bob Dole to challenge Clinton for the presidency in 1996. And once again, Ross Perot entered the race as a third-party candidate.

As earlier, Republicans focused on what they called Clinton's character flaws. But with the U.S. economy improving, more Americans found they could pay their bills and have money left over to save or invest. Investment opportunities flourished, especially within high-tech industries. The Clinton campaign emphasized that many Americans were better off than before Clinton took office.

Voters decided to give Clinton another chance and elected him to a second term. However, the vote was not an overwhelming mandate. Election results showed the lowest voter turnout for a presidential election since 1924—less than 50 percent of qualified voters cast ballots. Clinton received 45.6 million votes and 379 electoral votes, compared with Dole's 37.8 million votes and 159 electoral votes. Perot won 7.9 million votes.

Still, Clinton's election was a landmark. He was the first Democrat to win a second term since 1944. Moreover, Clinton became the only Democratic president to achieve two terms with another party controlling Congress. Voters chose to keep a Republican Congress, reelecting members in the same balance as the previous election.

Republican candidate Bob Dole *(left)* and Democratic candidate President Bill Clinton *(right)* shake hands on October 6, 1996, during the season's first **PRESIDENTIAL DEBATE**.

BILL CLINTON CELEBRATES HIS VICTORY in the 1996 presidential election with *(from left to right)* his wife, Hillary, vice president Al Gore, and Gore's wife, Tipper.

■ THE NATION AS GUARDIAN

Despite continuing problems at home, foreign policy dominated much of President Clinton's administrations. The American public took more of an interest in global issues too. The world seemed smaller due to computers and expanding business overseas. What happened overseas affected the daily lives of average Americans. Throughout the decade, the United States found itself involved in several conflicts around the globe.

■ BREAKUP OF YUGOSLAVIA

Ethnic battles emerged in the nation of Yugoslavia during Clinton's presidency. After World War II (1939–1945), six Eastern European republics had united under the Communist Yugoslav banner. But after the country's strong leader Tito died in 1980, unity in the region began to dissolve. An economic crisis in the late 1980s increased nationalist tensions. In 1991 and 1992, Croatia, Slovenia, Macedonia, and Bosnia-Herzegovina declared independence, while Serbia and Montenegro remained Yugoslav states. Almost immediately, civil wars broke out. Populations divided according to religious, ethnic, and linguistic lines, and leaders jockeyed for control.

Serbian president Slobodan Milosevic encouraged civil war among his neighbors. Using the force of the Yugoslav army, he fought to gather all ethnically Serbian regions under Serbia's control. He claimed this was to build a greater Serbia. But the real aim was to force non-Serbians from their homes. This became known as ethnic cleansing, a practice that brought death and destruction to the region.

In 1991 ethnic tensions in Bosnia-Herzegovina boiled over. Bosnia's population of 4.3 million people included 30 percent Serbs, 17 percent Croatians, and 45 percent Bosnian Muslims. Milosevic's allies began attacks to rid the country of Bosnian Muslims. Serb soldiers shot unarmed civilians, dumped them into mass graves, and destroyed businesses and mosques (Islamic houses of worship).

Terrified Muslims fled Bosnia. Some were corralled in Serbian-run detention camps. In August 1992, chilling images and tales of murder, destruction, and rape reached the U.S. news. President Bush protested to the United Nations but feared that sending U.S. soldiers into battle might hurt him politically.

By the time Clinton became president in 1993, the situation had worsened. UN forces tried to separate the warring factions and protect Bosnian Muslims. Countries of the North Atlantic Treaty Organization (NATO), a military alliance of democratic European and North American nations including the United States, banned sales of weapons to the region. But the ban meant Muslims could not protect themselves from well-armed Serbs. By late 1993, more than two hundred thousand people had died in Bosnia and Croatia, and tens of thousands of women had been raped. Countless others suffered torture in camps.

In 1995 NATO launched three days of air strikes, led by U.S. fighter planes, on Serbian military positions. Another fourteen days of air strikes followed. Meanwhile, Croatian forces successfully retook Croatian land occupied by

Bosnian Muslims and Croatians at a **BOSNIAN DETENTION CAMP** in Bosnia-Herzegovina in 1992. Reports of horrifying abuse eventually prompted the United States to lead a NATO effort to protect innocent citizens in the former Yugoslavia.

President Clinton shakes hands in 1996 with **U.S. SOLDIERS STATIONED IN BOSNIA-HERZEGOVINA** as part of NATO peacekeeping forces.

Serbs since 1991. Under increasing pressure, Milosevic joined Bosnian leaders in agreeing to a cease-fire and peace talks.

Leaders gathered in Dayton, Ohio, in November 1995. Milosevic finally guaranteed borders of Macedonia, Croatia, and Bosnia. In December he and other leaders signed the Dayton Accord. This agreement allowed peacekeepers to secure the region. The United States sent twenty thousand soldiers to Bosnia as part of the NATO peacekeeping force.

Several years later, another conflict in Serbia merited U.S. intervention. In 1998 ethnic Albanians living in Kosovo, a small province in southern Serbia, launched an uprising. They were determined to regain independence for Kosovo, which had been under Milosevic's dictatorship since 1989. Serbian police and military responded with brutal force. A new round of ethnic cleansing ensued, driving out or killing up to half of Kosovo's ethnic Albanians. Many families fled to neighboring Albania and Macedonia.

Backed by NATO, U.S. forces resumed air strikes in Serbia in March 1999. Bombs hit Belgrade, the capital, and Milosevic's party headquarters and home. Punishing air strikes lasted for seventy-nine days. By June Milosevic finally agreed to NATO demands and Serbian forces left Kosovo. The UN and NATO sent a peacekeeping force of forty-eight thousand to protect Kosovo.

President Clinton praised the U.S. role in the Kosovo peace process. In an

> **"America is a nation with global interests and responsibilities. Some may find that a burden, but for most Americans, it is a source of great pride."**

—*Madeleine K. Albright, then U.S. ambassador to the United Nations, 1995*

address from the Oval Office, he thanked U.S. armed forces "for their superb performance" and the nation's people "for their stand against ethnic cleansing and their generous support of the refugees, many of whom had come to America."

■ AFRICA

New threats surfaced in several African countries during the 1990s. Different factions battled for control in Somalia, Rwanda, and the Democratic Republic of the Congo. Television news fed Americans steady reports of famine, killing, and forced evacuations. But the U.S. government was selective about which conflicts it entered.

Warring tribes had long kept Somalia a trouble spot. In 1990 antigovernment movements flared into bloody civil war. Problems escalated when the nation experienced widespread drought. As the drought and resulting famine persisted, the government descended into chaos.

UN relief efforts in Somalia were problematic. Two years into the civil war, relief workers still couldn't distribute food and medical supplies amid the chaos and violence. About 350,000 Somalis were dead, and more were dying.

In December 1992, the United States sent twenty-eight thousand troops to Somalia. Their job was to ensure the safety of workers distributing supplies. President Bush dubbed the mission Operation Restore Hope.

An aid worker with **OPERATION RESTORE HOPE** vaccinates a Somali child in 1992. U.S. troops helped protect aid workers in Somalia.

Somali warlords shot down this **U.S. BLACKHAWK HELICOPTER** over Mogadishu on October 3, 1993.

At first the U.S. presence calmed tensions, and warring leaders agreed to discuss peace with UN representatives. But on October 3, 1993, the fragile peace shattered with a brutal ambush of U.S. soldiers in the capital city of Mogadishu. U.S. Army Rangers sent to capture a Somali warlord found themselves under heavy fire from his lieutenants. When a U.S. Blackhawk helicopter was gunned down, soldiers were surrounded and outnumbered ten to one. They remained trapped in battle for seventeen hours before an armored rescue force could move in. After fighting ended, eighteen U.S. soldiers lay dead and eighty-four were wounded.

The attack proved a terrible blow to the United States. Thereafter, public and government support for the mission waned. U.S. troops pulled out by the following March, and the UN withdrew workers a year later. But clan warfare continued as severe flooding and more drought produced further hardship.

In the south central African nation of Rwanda, savage ethnic violence erupted in 1994 between the Hutu and Tutsi people. The Tutsi made up just 15 percent of the population. But they held a much larger share of the nation's wealth and political power, causing tension between the two groups.

In April 1994, a plane crash, caused by rocket fire, killed the Hutu president of Rwanda and the president of Burundi. Their deaths triggered a murder spree. Hutus were responsible for most of the violence. During one hundred days, more than eight hundred thousand Tutsi and their Hutu supporters were slaughtered, mostly by machete. The massacre displaced another three million people.

> ## "The failure to try to stop Rwanda's tragedies became one of the greatest tragedies of my presidency."
>
> *—Bill Clinton, reflecting on his presidency, 2004*

The memory of humiliation in Somalia lingered in the minds of U.S. government leaders. As a result, the United States condemned the violence in Rwanda but took no action to stop the killings. By July 1994, Tutsi forces had captured the capital city and victoriously declared a cease-fire. Many Hutus fled to the neighboring Democratic Republic of Congo. Ethnic tensions and violence in the region continued into the twenty-first century.

"With a few thousand troops and help from our allies . . . , we could have saved lives," Clinton later wrote. "The failure to try to stop Rwanda's tragedies became one of the greatest tragedies of my presidency."

■ BUILDING PEACE

President Clinton helped broker two breakthrough peace agreements. The first was between Palestinians and Israeli Jews in the Middle East. Both groups—Arab Palestinians and Israeli Jews—laid claim to ancient Palestine, the modern country of Israel. The state of Israel had been established as a Jewish homeland in 1948. Ever since, Palestinians had struggled with Israel for rights and control of land through a series of wars as well as violent and nonviolent resistance.

Earlier U.S. presidents had helped move these groups toward a peace agreement. In 1993 President Clinton revived peace talks by inviting Israeli prime minister Yitzhak Rabin and Palestine Liberation Organization (PLO) leader Yasser Arafat to meet in Oslo, Norway. The talks resulted in the first stages of an agreement, the Oslo Accords, which determined a timetable for restoring Palestinian self-rule in the Israeli-occupied Gaza Strip and West Bank. Israel hoped to exchange those lands for peaceful relations with Palestinians.

Then in November 1995, an Israeli extremist assassinated Rabin. He resented Rabin's negotiations with Palestinians. After the more conservative Benjamin Netanyahu became prime minister of Israel, the peace process stalled

President Bill Clinton *(center)* oversaw a **PEACE AGREEMENT** between Israeli prime minister
Yitzhak Rabin *(left)* and PLO leader Yasser Arafat *(right)* in September 1993.

once again. In 1998 President Clinton invited Netanyahu and Arafat to a meeting in Wye Mills, Maryland, to resume negotiations. At the close of the decade, however, the Israeli-Palestinian conflict was still far from resolved.

In 1998 President Clinton managed a historic peace agreement in Northern Ireland, a part of the United Kingdom. Mistrust ran centuries deep between the Nationalists, who were mostly Catholics, and the Unionists, who were mostly Protestants. Catholics wanted Northern Ireland to become one nation with the independent Republic of Ireland, while Protestants' loyalty lay with the United Kingdom. Fighting and terrorism had been the source of much bloodshed.

Clinton joined British prime minister Tony Blair and representatives of each faction in negotiations that lasted twenty-two months. In the final days, Clinton encouraged a settlement by promising U.S. support if the two sides agreed to lasting peace. Leaders from each party signed the Good Friday Accord on April 10, 1998. Passage of the landmark accord ended thirty years of fighting that cost more than three thousand lives.

■ TERRORISM AGAINST THE UNITED STATES

Isolated acts of terrorism against the United States shocked the nation in the 1990s. On February 26, 1993, a bomb exploded in the garage underneath New York's World Trade Center. The blast tore through three stories of concrete, setting off a fire that released suffocating smoke. The impact also blew a hole in the ceiling of an underground train station below the garage, crushing travelers waiting for a train. Most of the 110,000 people who worked and visited the center each day escaped. But 6 people died, and 1,042 required medical attention. The bombing devastated the nation. "We all have that feeling of being violated," explained New York governor Mario Cuomo.

Police and the FBI immediately began investigating who might have been responsible for the blast. Four months later, a judge sentenced four Islamic extremists to life for the bombing. Sheikh Omar Abdel Rahman, a blind cleric (religious leader) with ties to al-Qaeda, an Islamic militant group, received the same sentence for masterminding the plan. Militant Islamic extremists wanted to punish the United States, in part for its support of Israel, a historic enemy of Arab nations, many of which share the region's dominant religion of Islam.

On February 26, 1993, Islamic terrorists bombed an underground garage of New York City's **WORLD TRADE CENTER**. Below, victims are treated for injuries.

Terrorists lashed out at the United States on August 7, 1998. The explosions from the **BOMBING OF THE U.S. EMBASSY** in Nairobi, Kenya, killed 258 people, including 12 Americans, and injured more than 5,000 others.

On August 7, 1998, terrorists attacked Americans again. This time, they bombed U.S. embassies in the African cities of Nairobi, Kenya, and Dar es Salaam, Tanzania. Investigations into the tragedy pointed again to al-Qaeda and its leader, the wealthy Osama bin Laden. In 1996 al-Qaeda had issued a Declaration of War against the United States. Bin Laden was offended by U.S. troops stationed in Saudi Arabia during the 1991 Persian Gulf War. Saudi Arabia is his native land and the birthplace of Islam. Investigators believe that bin Laden funded the manufacture of the bombs and paid for terrorist training camps in Afghanistan.

President Clinton ordered missile attacks on suspected terrorist targets. On August 20, 1998, U.S. planes dropped bombs on a terrorist training complex in Afghanistan and on a plant thought to manufacture weapons in Khartoum, Sudan. (In fact, it was a pharmaceutical factory.) Three years later, four men were tried and convicted for their roles in the embassy bombings.

■ A PRESIDENT UNDER ATTACK

While foreign policy matters demanded President Clinton's attention, storms were brewing at home. Paula Jones sued the president in 1994 for sexual harassment while she was an Arkansas state government worker. At the trial, begun in 1997, lawyers uncovered other Clinton affairs that proved damaging.

At 9:02 A.M. on April 19, 1995, the second anniversary of the Waco siege in Texas, tragedy struck Oklahoma City, Oklahoma. A bomb-filled truck exploded in front of the downtown Alfred P. Murrah Federal Building *(right)*. The explosion blew out the front of the nine-story office building, killing 168 people and injuring about 600 more.

Police Sergeant Jerry Flowers remembered the scene as he entered the building: "Black smoke was shooting in the air. . . . Everywhere I looked was blood, misery, and pain. . . . I've never seen so much pain, both physical and emotional."

Within a few days, the FBI tracked down Persian Gulf War veteran Timothy McVeigh as a suspect. The FBI found McVeigh in jail. Police had arrested him shortly after the bombing for driving without license plates and carrying a hidden weapon. But they had no idea what he had just done.

McVeigh proudly declared his membership in an antigovernment militia group. He hated the U.S. government and the way FBI agents had handled the Waco incident. McVeigh's partners in the bombing were Terry Nichols, who helped plan and prepare for the attack, and a third man, Michael Fortier, who had been aware of the plan and cooperated with officials in exchange for a lighter sentence. After years of trials, Nichols went to jail for life. And for his act of violence—at the time, the deadliest terrorist attack in the country's history— McVeigh was found guilty and executed in June 2001. His was the first federal execution since 1963.

The media ran a rash of stories delving into Clinton's private life. One more recent affair involved Monica Lewinsky, a twenty-one-year-old White House intern. Under oath, Clinton said he had never had a relationship with this woman. He also went on television to deny the sexual affair.

Affairs are not against the law, but lying to a judge under oath is. After proof of the affair surfaced, Clinton admitted in August 1998 that he had lied, apologizing on television to Americans. A special prosecutor pressed the president about his lies and about telling the intern to lie for him in court. Republican lawmakers called for Clinton's impeachment—to charge someone with misconduct while in office—for lying under oath and trying to obstruct the Jones case.

A photographer snapped this shot of **BILL CLINTON HUGGING MONICA LEWINSKY** the day after Clinton was reelected to the White House in 1996. News of their affair and the cover-up haunted Clinton to the end of his presidency.

The House of Representatives narrowly voted to impeach the president on counts of perjury (lying under oath) and obstruction of justice in December 1998. The impeachment trial, held in the Senate, began the following January. Senate Republicans were unable to rally the two-thirds majority needed to remove the president. Clinton had endured public embarrassment, but he escaped losing his presidency.

Many Americans believed Clinton had shown terrible moral judgment. But they disliked the media and Republican witch hunt, especially the invasion of privacy. Journalist Kenneth Walsh summed up the Clinton ordeal this way: "In a *U.S. News and World Report* poll, respondents said they were 'disgusted' by the scandal. Everything about it: the players, the politics, the partisanship, the policy put on hold while the scandal ground on. And, contrary to the pop [critics], those surveyed said they didn't believe there would be a lasting scar, that the nation's moral fiber would fray, or that it would spawn a generation of liars."

■ THE CLINTON LEGACY

In June 1999, Vice President Al Gore announced his run for the presidency on the 2000 Democratic ticket. His Republican opponent would be George W. Bush, son of former President Bush. By then voters had tired of Clinton scandals. Gore would have an uphill battle trying to separate himself from the Clinton drama.

Yet Americans were prospering. Whatever Clinton's choices in his personal life, he left a booming economy and largely peaceful foreign relations. Time would tell which of his successes or failures would define his presidency in public memory. The decade ended with a nation clearly better off than when it began.

A businessman types on his LAPTOP COMPUTER while commuting to work in 1992. Advances in technology allowed people of the 1990s to work on the go.

CHAPTER THREE

A WHOLE NEW AGE:
COMMUNICATIONS, SCIENCE, AND TECHNOLOGY

New inventions transformed lives during the nineties. Individuals and businesses communicated in totally different ways from the previous decade. Generation X, the teens and young adults of the 1990s (also known as GenXers), became the first computer generation and the first age group to navigate with cell phones glued to their ears.

The 1990s also saw unimaginable discoveries in medical science. Medical advances created and extended life as technology opened doors to better health care. And while scientists experimented with how to improve life on Earth, astronauts continued to explore space. This was a time of exciting innovation.

■ COMPUTER ADVANCES

Some Americans had been using basic computers at work and at home since the late 1970s. By the nineties, upgraded computers allowed information to travel at lightning speed with the click of a mouse. New operating systems, such as Microsoft Windows 3.0 (released in 1990) and Windows 95 (1995), improved user-friendliness and integrated more software programs. So many computer manufacturers installed Windows 95 that after its introduction, the Microsoft Corporation dominated the industry. But by 1999, Apple Computer had reclaimed a portion of the market with its new, colorful iMac and iBook computers.

43

Improved operating systems and hardware paired with lower prices meant average citizens could join the computer revolution. By the end of the decade, 42.1 percent of U.S. households owned computers. Parents documented the family's finances on spreadsheets. Students typed homework using word processors. Adults conducted business from home through modems. Children and adults vied for computer time to play video games.

Computer use skyrocketed in 1992 with growing use of the Internet. The Department of Defense originally devised a network of linked computers, called ARPANET, in the late 1960s and early 1970s as a substitute communication system in case of nuclear attack. The concept remained mainly limited to a government network until 1989, when British software developer Tim Berners-Lee began creating the World Wide Web. He devised standardized codes that gave computers an address and allowed them to link, interpret, and display "pages" of media. He made his creation available on the growing electronic network, the Internet, in 1991.

The Web transformed the personal computer into a means of communication and source of information, and the amount of material stored online exploded. By 1999 individuals had access to more than 800 million Web pages. Online encyclopedias, newspapers, and magazines were a convenient way to read the latest news, find answers to health and dating questions, or discover sports scores. Library catalogs, converted from paper files to online listings, required only a simple online search to find books and resources. By 1999 more than one-third of U.S. households were wired into the Internet. Computers with Web browsers and an Internet connection became fixtures in businesses and schools.

TIM BERNERS-LEE is the brain behind the World Wide Web. Berners-Lee *(pictured here in the late 1990s)* later became the director of the World Wide Web Consortium, which is sponsored in the United States by the Massachusetts Institute of Technology in Cambridge, Massachusetts.

The success of William Henry Gates III, or Bill Gates, is legendary. Growing up in Seattle, Washington, Gates found his passion in the 1960s when his school provided time on a primitive computer—then brand-new technology—for its students. When he was thirteen, Gates wrote his first software program. It allowed people to play tic-tac-toe with the computer.

Gates and three of his classmates lost their computer privileges after they hacked into the operating system to extend their computer time. This incident led the managing company, Computer Center Corporation, to hire the boys to get the bugs out of their program. At seventeen years old, Gates and his friend Paul Allen created their own company called Traf-O-Data.

As a student at Harvard University, Gates continued to write computer programs. He believed that "the computer would be a valuable tool on every office desktop and in every home."

Gates quit college in his third year to devote himself to the company he and Allen started, which they renamed Microsoft in 1976. Four years later, International Business Machines (IBM), a leader in computer hardware, hired Microsoft to write a program for its new personal computer. MS-DOS became an instant hit, catapulting Microsoft and Gates into the big leagues of the industry. (Allen left the company in 1983.)

Under Gates's leadership, Microsoft

BILL GATES saw the possibilities of computers in the marketplace, which led him to found Microsoft.

continued to grow and improve its programs. In 1990 Microsoft released Windows 3.0, the third incarnation of the popular Windows operating system. This version offered advanced graphics, sixteen colors and more power. With each improved version of Windows, more computer manufacturers acquired the rights to use it. By 1991 Gates presided over an empire that earned $462 million in that year alone. He had become one of the wealthiest people in the world by the end of the decade.

Gates uses his resources to benefit others. In 1994 he and his wife started the Bill and Melinda Gates Foundation. It funds initiatives in global health and learning. Gates also wrote two books, *The Road Ahead* (1995) and *Business @ the Speed of Thought* (1999). Profits from these books go to organizations that educate people in computer skill development.

Throughout the 1990s, the Internet expanded to include bulletin boards and chat rooms. Electronic mail, or e-mail, allowed people to send messages instantly and easily. Traditional mail became known as snail mail, taking days to reach its destination. The Internet offered the ability to pay bills online, manage investments, or play games.

Friends online at the same time quickly took to instant messaging. With instant messaging, buddies could exchange messages in "real time" as they typed them. At first, only those using the same Internet software, such as America Online, could "IM"—chat via instant message. Internet-wide instant messaging was possible within several years. Millions of people enjoyed chatting with faraway friends and family without the cost of long-distance phone calls.

Critics complained that Internet communities reduced real community and real interaction. Employees spent most of their days sitting in a chair looking at a computer monitor. At home they checked e-mail and joined chat groups. Some worried that the more computers connected humans, the more they kept people disconnected in the physical world.

Others disliked the unfiltered nature of Web content. Anyone could post their opinions or provide information. Web pages offering high-quality academic information or news were mixed in with those featuring unedited, inaccurate, and biased content. Spam crowded e-mail in-boxes, ranging from unsolicited ads to scams and viruses.

Uncensored cyberspace also presented new threats. Increasingly, sexual predators in chat rooms found the Internet the perfect place to seek out

"The Internet was virtually lawless; no one owned it, no one controlled it, and those who used it answered to no set of rules. . . . Information was free and all voices were equal, or as a *New Yorker* cartoon quipped, 'On the Internet, nobody knows you're a dog.'"

—*Peter Jennings, author and newscaster, 1998*

and develop relationships with unsuspecting targets. As a result, Internet monitoring and filtering software was developed to help parents and librarians protect kids online. Education about such dangers helped young people protect themselves.

■ UNTETHERED COMMUNICATION

During the 1980s, most telephones were connected by a cord to a phone jack in the wall. Even cordless phones lost reception if they were too far from the base that was plugged into the jack. Not much changed after Motorola introduced the first wireless mobile phone to the public in 1983. The first cellular phones were expensive, clunky, shoe-sized devices. These were mainly reserved for emergencies and important business.

In 1990 the first mobile phone using digital technology hit the market. These units were smaller, easier to handle, and provided clearer calls at farther distances. Gradually, family, friends, and coworkers adapted to being only a call away. Cell phones revolutionized the telephone industry and 1990s culture. Phone ringing and conversations became common on buses, in shopping malls and theaters, and even in classes.

As newer models hit the market, phone prices and size came down. In 1984 stores sold a total of twenty-five thousand cell phones. By 2000 sales had exploded to more than one million cell phones per week.

■ COMPUTERSPEAK

One offshoot of frequent e-mail and instant messaging was condensed language. The less formal nature of e-mail meant communication often

Christopher Galvin, chief executive officer of Motorola, talks on a **CELL PHONE** made by his company. Motorola led the cell phone industry in the 1990s.

omitted the formal greetings, language, and formatting that writers usually included in snail mail. For example, e-mail senders paid less attention to punctuation and capitalization. Some viewed Internet communication as the end of good writing.

The new medium gave rise to a host of changes in spelling, vocabulary, and grammar. Initials and abbreviations replaced standard language. Teenagers and young adults quickly adopted and shaped this shorthand jargon. Some common terms became standard for e-mails and instant messages:

brb: be right back   omg: oh my god
btw: by the way   pos: parent over shoulder
fyi: for your information rotfl: rolling on the floor laughing
kpc: keep parents clueless ttfn: ta-ta for now
lol: laugh out loud   ttyl: talk to you later

■ THE DIGITAL AGE

Digital technology expanded into other time-saving and entertaining gadgets. Digital processes involve turning information—sound, images, or words—into bits, or bytes. The bits are translated on a computer screen or transmitted via satellite and tiny fiber-optic lines. Digital technology was the driving force behind so many new inventions that Time-Life Books named the nineties the digital decade.

Personal digital assistants, or PDAs, such as Palm Pilots gained popularity in 1996 to help users organize their lives with a hand-held computer the size of a deck of cards. These devices stored appointments, to-do lists, and phone numbers. By the end of the decade, they could wirelessly access e-mail. Many students and businesspeople relied on their digital calendars so much that they were lost without them.

In the late 1990s, digital cameras altered how people take and share pictures. They began replacing traditional cameras, which use rolls of film to be developed

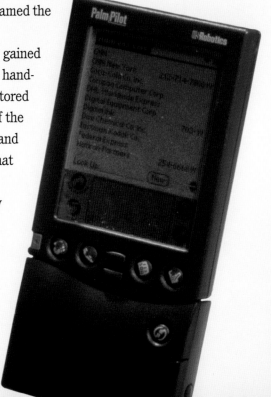

PERSONAL DIGITAL ASSISTANTS (PDAs), such as this Palm Pilot, came onto the market in the 1990s. They helped busy people keep track of their social schedules.

Theodore Kaczynski *(right in orange jumpsuit)* was determined to single-handedly stop the march of technology. Born in Chicago, Illinois, in 1942, Kaczynski was a highly intelligent student with poor social skills. He entered Harvard University at sixteen years old, earned a PhD in mathematics, and became an assistant math professor at the University of California–Berkeley by the age of twenty-five. But he quit teaching to move into a primitive, isolated cabin in Lincoln, Montana, in 1971. There he plotted to derail technological advances by scaring off the experts and leaders of large institutions that support them. From 1978 to 1995, he sent sixteen letter bombs to professors and others who were connected with the technology industry. The FBI dubbed him the Unabomber after the places that received the bombs: *un*iversities and *a*irlines.

One of Kaczynski's trademarks was writing long tirades against the "onslaught of technology." He sent them to newspapers to gain attention and to scare a worried public.

A manifesto by the Unabomber was published in the *New York Times* and *Washington Post* on September 19, 1995. The papers hoped that a reader would help identify him. Indeed, his brother recognized his writing and contacted the FBI, leading to his capture. By then explosions from the Unabomber's sixteen letter bombs had killed three people and injured twenty-three. He received life imprisonment without parole.

49

in darkrooms. Traditional photography requires shooting a roll of twenty-four or thirty-six photos and paying to have it developed into negatives and prints. Only after developing—which could take an hour or several days—would someone see the photos for the first time. In digital cameras, a tiny memory card holds as many photos as several film rolls. The camera can be connected directly to a computer for viewing, editing, and uploading. People can shoot countless photos without worrying about the cost of using and developing film. And through e-mail and websites, distributing photos became easier and cheaper than ever before.

Computers, the Internet, cell phones with voice mail, and digital cameras made old ways of communicating outdated by the end of the decade. "Just think about how people 'work' these days," wrote Scott Savage in *Plain* magazine. "They sit in a chair and stare at a machine." But for most people, the benefits far outweighed the drawbacks of the digital age.

■ HUMAN GENOME PROJECT

New medical technology allowed for breakthrough research and advances in medical science. In 1990 the U.S. government funded one of the most exciting endeavors in this field, the Human Genome Project. The Department of Energy and the National Institutes of Health coordinated this fifteen-year project to sequence the estimated twenty thousand genes in the human body.

A genome consists of the entire genetic makeup of an organism. A person's unique genome is determined by the combination of genes inherited from each parent at conception. Genes hold information for making the proteins that help to determine an individual's traits. They affect appearance, personality, and growth and development. These influential genes are made up of sequences of chemical pairs along strands of deoxyribonucleic acid (DNA). In all, three billion pairs of chemicals form the human genome that is contained in the nucleus of nearly every cell of the body.

The Human Genome Project progressed so well that researchers roughly mapped the entire human genome by the year 2000, five years ahead of schedule. Their results pinpointed locations of various genes on chromosomes

A researcher cleans glass plates used in genetic sequencing. The **HUMAN GENOME PROJECT** sought to map out the genes in human DNA.

(DNA-containing structures). Encouraged, scientists studied genes in search of mutations that may lead to illness. Although much remains to be done, researchers were able to identify certain harmful mutations, such as one causing Huntington's disease. Scientists hope to be able one day to manipulate genes and turn off mechanisms that cause diseases and disabilities.

■ DOLLY THE SHEEP

During the spring of 1996, Dr. Ian Wilmut, a Scottish scientist, achieved an astonishing feat. He created a lamb from a single cell of an adult sheep (the parent animal). Wilmut and his scientists had replaced the nucleus of a sheep egg cell with the genetic material from the adult cell. They then planted the embryo inside a surrogate (substitute) mother, where it grew to term. The resulting lamb was a clone, or copy, of the parent animal, with the exact same genetic makeup. They called her Dolly.

Dolly the sheep was not the first cloned animal. In 1952 scientists had cloned a tadpole and experimented with reproducing embryo cells. But Dolly was the first animal cloned from an adult cell. Scientists had known since 1981 that certain cells from animal embryos, called embryonic stem cells, have the ability to develop into any type of body cell. But researchers believed that once a stem cell developed into a bone, heart, or other type of cell, its role was permanent. After the successful cloning of Dolly, they understood that reprogramming was possible.

The scientific community and public hailed the event as a significant breakthrough. The ability to create life in a laboratory opened many possibilities.

Born on July 6, 1996, **DOLLY THE SHEEP** was the first mammal cloned from the embryonic stem cells of an adult sheep. She lived to be six years old.

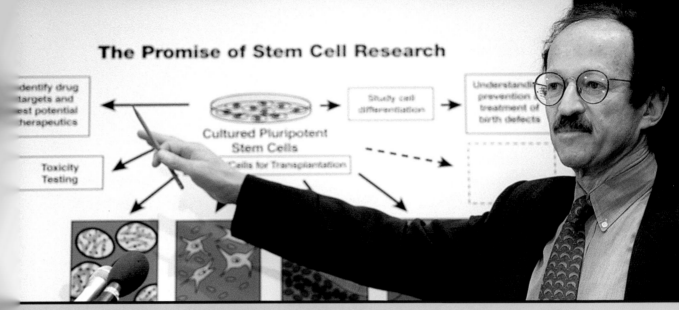

The Promise of Stem Cell Research

- Identify drug targets and test potential therapeutics
- Toxicity Testing
- Cultured Pluripotent Stem Cells
- Cells for Transplantation
- Study cell differentiation
- Understanding prevention and treatment of birth defects

In 1998 Dr. Harold Varmus of the National Institutes of Health showed the potential for medical breakthroughs using **STEM CELL RESEARCH**. Opponents of stem cell research worry about creating a demand for embryos for the purpose of research rather than reproduction.

Endangered species could be preserved. Prize farm animals could be reproduced. Politicians and scientists grappled with the ethical questions of cloning as other scientists scrambled to reproduce Wilmut's success.

■ STEM CELL RESEARCH

Scientists wondered if human embryonic stem cells—like those of other animals—could be grown into specialized adult cells, as in muscle tissue, blood, or bone marrow. If so, this would provide new possibilities for treating and curing disease. Healthy new tissue could be grown to replace diseased or damaged tissue. In 1998 two teams of researchers grew embryonic stem cells into several different types of adult cells, proving the potential of this field.

Scientists believed embryonic stem cells held greater promise for medical treatment than specific adult cells did. (Adult stem cells in bone marrow, for example, can become new blood cells but cannot be used to grow a new liver.) But experimenting with human embryos caused great controversy. The opposition believed that life begins at conception, when the egg is fertilized. For them, any use of embryos interferes with formation of a future human. Proponents of the research argued that stem cell therapy used leftover embryos in fertility clinics—extras not used in in vitro (fertilizing eggs in a lab to foster pregnancy) fertilization—which would be discarded anyway.

President Clinton supported this research, even though many in Congress did not. But he agreed that limits should specify what scientists could and could not do. "I think we cannot walk away from the potential to save lives and improve lives, to help people literally get up and walk, to do all kinds of things we could never have imagined," he said, "as long as we meet rigorous ethical standards."

■ STARGAZING

While medical scientists grappled with life on Earth, astronomers and astronauts explored space. In 1990 the National Aeronautics and Space Administration (NASA) launched the Hubble Space Telescope into orbit around Earth from the space shuttle *Discovery*. The space-based observatory allowed astronomers to examine the solar system in ways never before possible. Hubble's advanced sensors could focus on a target for up to twenty-four hours while orbiting Earth at 17,500 miles (28,000 km) per hour. The Hubble proved so powerful that astronomers witnessed the universe beyond Earth's galaxy for the first time.

Hubble observations changed astronomers' understanding of the planets, our Milky Way galaxy, and distant galaxies. In 1994 the telescope photographed the comet Shoemaker-Levy 9 as it crashed into Jupiter. In 1998 NASA astronomers discovered from Hubble data that the expansion of the universe is not slowing, as some had thought, but actually speeding up. Evidence lay in measurements of

Powerful cameras aboard the **HUBBLE SPACE TELESCOPE** took this picture of a dying star. Images sent back from the Hubble gave scientists a new view of astronomical activity outside of our solar system. The stunning photos also generated the general public's interest in the U.S. space program.

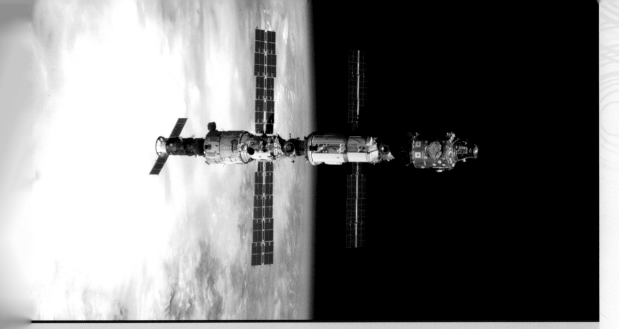

THE INTERNATIONAL SPACE STATION is seen in orbit above Earth in September 2000. The ISS was begun in the 1990s, but the first crew did not arrive for a stay until 2000.

ancient exploding stars called supernovae, too far away to be seen by any ground telescope. The next year, astronomers used Hubble measurements from eighteen galaxies to estimate that the universe is twelve to fourteen billion years old.

The nineties also saw the launch of the International Space Station (ISS). A space-based station allows astronauts to examine Earth and its atmosphere in new ways, study how space conditions affect living things, and more. The ISS was the first station designed, built, and used by multiple space agencies around the globe. Russian and U.S. spacecraft carried the first parts of the station into space in 1998. Delivery and assembly of additional parts continued well into the 2000s. By late 2000, the ISS was ready to house its first full-time crew.

■ ENVIRONMENTAL AWARENESS

Experts in the 1990s identified global warming—an increase in Earth's average temperature—as a major threat to life. Scientists believed that the cause of this warming trend is increased concentrations of carbon dioxide and other greenhouse gases in the atmosphere. These gases keep Earth comfortably warm by letting in radiation from the sun and trapping it as heat, as the glass in a greenhouse does. But higher levels of these gases, due to emissions and pollution from homes, cars, and industry, cause more heat to be trapped. In addition, scientists found that some polluting gases burned holes in the protective ozone layer of Earth's atmosphere. Ozone shields the planet from the sun's harmful ultraviolet rays. Without it, those rays can damage the environment.

The 1990s became the warmest recorded decade, with five years of the decade topping the charts. The warming trend triggered extreme storms and drought and caused sections of coastal Antarctic ice shelves to melt and break off. The Arctic's year-round ice cap shrank as more of it melted each summer. Glaciers around the world began to shrink at a rapid rate. Scientists worried that if warming continued, oceans would rise enough to flood large coastal regions.

Although Americans showed concern for the environment, many were reluctant to alter their lives greatly. Businesses especially were hesitant to make expensive changes to their operations to become more Earth friendly. President George H. W. Bush signed the Clean Air Act in 1990 to improve air quality by limiting emissions. Some cities established recycling programs. But the nation showed little urgency in making significant changes, and some individuals denied that global warming was a problem.

As evidence of harmful climate change piled up, the environment became an important issue worldwide. Representatives from 160 nations met in Kyoto, Japan, in 1997 to discuss ways to reduce greenhouse gases. President Clinton attended and agreed to reduce 1990 U.S. emission levels 7 percent by 2012. But Congress refused to sign the Kyoto Protocol and commit to the reduction. Big-business interests convinced lawmakers that the cost of switching to cleaner practices would hurt the economy. However, environmental awareness and popular demand for Earth-friendly practices and products grew steadily as the decade came to a close.

Changes in Earth's climate have been linked to **GLOBAL WARMING**. These satellite photos from 1979 *(left)* and 2007 *(right)* show the decrease in Arctic sea ice around Greenland. Scientists and researchers in the 1990s began tracking climate models to document the effects of global warming.

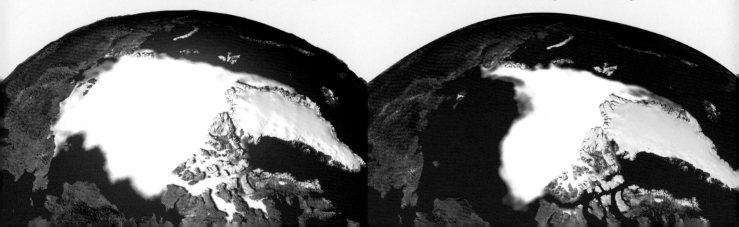

Students at the University of Michigan in Ann Arbor protest U.S. corporations that send labor overseas to countries with lower wages. EXPORTING JOBS OVERSEAS meant a loss of jobs in the United States, contributing to the economic downturn of the 1990s.

CHAPTER FOUR

FROM BUST TO BOOM:
THE SEESAW ECONOMY OF THE 1990s

In the early 1990s, the U.S. economy was experiencing a downturn. Businesses slashed an average of twenty-four hundred jobs every workday. Many losses were due to overseas competition. Several nations around the world had recently freed their economy from strict government control. This allowed their businesses to join the global market for the first time.

U.S. companies seeking less expensive ways to make their products could find cheap labor in China, India, and countries in Central and South America and Eastern Europe. Companies in foreign countries invited U.S. corporations to contract with local businesses to produce goods for a fraction of what they cost to make at home.

Factory workers in the United States began losing jobs at increasing rates beginning in the 1980s. The trend continued into the 1990s. Historically, the national economy often had periods of downturn in which fewer jobs were available. But the United States always recovered and hiring began again. This time was different. Moving production overseas meant jobs would be permanently lost to Americans.

Equally troubling, the jobs left for U.S. workers did not pay as well. One study reported that "two-thirds of workers who lost jobs in manufacturing industries hit by overseas competition earned less on their next job." One-quarter of those who found new employment saw their income drop by 30 percent

HOW FAR WOULD A DOLLAR GO in the 1990s?

	1990s	2000s (first decade)
Average U.S. worker's income	$34,890	$35,000

TYPICAL PRICES

First-class stamp	32¢	44¢
Candy bar	50¢	75¢
Loaf of bread	69¢	$2.79
Gallon of milk	$2.96	$2.99
Movie ticket	$4.46	$9.00
Man's haircut	$15.00	$30.00
Pair of athletic shoes	$43.36	$79.99
Child's bicycle	$100.00	$139.99
Two-door car	$18,500	$20,000
Three-bedroom house	$158,700	$300,000

(Prices are samples only. At any given time, prices vary by year, location, size, brand, and model.)

or more. Families with lower incomes soon discovered they had difficulty covering their expenses.

Another difference in nineties *downsizing*, the corporate term for layoffs, was who lost their jobs. Downsizing hit a wider segment of the U.S. population than previous stretches of unemployment. At one time, white-collar management jobs were thought immune from firings. But these jobs were lost after high-level executives bought, sold, and merged companies to turn a quick profit. No employee, it seemed, could count on job security anymore.

Farmers experienced rough times too. Giant investment corporations saw agriculture as another business opportunity. Investors bought vast acres of farmland. Small family farms fell like dominoes as large businesses gathered them under one umbrella company. Owners of farms passed down through generations, unable to compete with big-business agriculture, auctioned off their goods. Farmworkers hunted for jobs in the nearest city.

Then presidential hopeful Bill Clinton *(right)* visits a community soup kitchen in 1992. **HIGH UNEMPLOYMENT** during the 1990s left many Americans struggling to make ends meet.

Loss of jobs at every level contributed to widespread personal debt. Families filed for bankruptcy at alarming rates. Debt increased on the national level as well. Continued military buildup and heavy government spending had contributed to more than $4 trillion in national debt.

President Bush faced record national debt and unemployment of about 10 percent. In some areas, such as inner cities, that figure jumped to 20 percent. In 1991 these figures reached a nine-year high.

■ REBOUNDING ECONOMY

President Bush's plan to raise taxes did little to relieve the problems before the end of his term. When President Clinton took office, the nation's broken economy needed serious mending. He instituted a financial package that included new taxes and ways to build business and create jobs.

Clinton's 1993 tax package aimed to reduce the deep debt he inherited and provide relief for those most in need. A final budget of spending cuts and higher taxes for large businesses and high-income individuals barely squeaked by in Congress. But it was a sound beginning. The budget cuts prompted a drop in interest rates. This in turn encouraged investment, which fueled national productivity. Tax cuts and investment incentives for small businesses stimulated their growth and generated millions of new jobs. Other initiatives gave tax credits for research and development, reformed student loans, and provided incentives to invest in struggling communities.

Clinton also supported the North American Free Trade Agreement (NAFTA), first negotiated under the Bush administration. NAFTA would remove trade barriers between the United States, Canada, and Mexico over the next fourteen years. Clinton felt NAFTA was good for the global market, as long as each country upheld labor and environmental standards. "I thought America had to support Mexico's economic growth to ensure long-term stability in our hemisphere," Clinton later said.

Republicans embraced NAFTA because it opened foreign markets to U.S. companies. But labor advocates and some business leaders feared U.S. companies could not compete against goods from nations that paid lower wages. They believed U.S. workers "would hear a giant sucking sound of jobs being drawn to Mexico." The vote on NAFTA passed in late 1993 with strong support of Republicans. But Clinton lost the support of many from his own party, particularly workers in southern textile mills and factories.

In 1999 a meeting of the World Trade Organization (WTO) revived controversy over international trade. As many as fifty thousand people flocked to Seattle, Washington, to protest the WTO Ministerial Conference. The WTO helps set rules for global trade. But protesters felt it undermined national laws that promote fair labor, environmental protection, and food safety, among other concerns. On November 30, 1999, the massive crowds blocked traffic and succeeded in disrupting the WTO meeting. Over the next three days,

George H. W. Bush *(left)* shakes hands with Mexican ambassador Gustavo Petricioli *(right)* after signing the **NORTH AMERICAN FREE TRADE AGREEMENT (NAFTA)** on December 17, 1992. NAFTA was signed into U.S. law after it was approved by Congress in 1993.

Protesters flocked to Seattle in an effort to disrupt a meeting of the **WORLD TRADE ORGANIZATION** there in 1999.

Seattle police and other law enforcement used tear gas to break up the crowds, and police arrested hundreds. A new national debate on globalization followed as Americans responded to the events in Seattle.

Nonetheless, Clinton's economic reform was seeing positive effects within several years. By the late 1990s, a technology boom was sweeping the nation, fueling profits and creating jobs.

■ TECHNOLOGY AS BIG BUSINESS

High-tech companies and e-commerce led the nation into economic improvement as computer-related businesses peaked during the 1990s. Entrepreneurs became wealthy quickly by creating new products only available online. Tech-savvy people were suddenly in high demand for companies that wanted to lead the way in Internet business.

Early companies to jump on the Internet-shopping bandwagon reaped huge rewards. Amazon.com, originally a site that sold books at reduced prices, and eBay, an online marketplace and auction site, popularized shopping by computer. Online shopping generated more than $8 billion in Internet sales during 1998, and purchases increased each year thereafter.

Individuals who invested in "dot-com" companies also benefited from these businesses' success. Profits from dot-com stocks gave investors additional income. This economic boost helped stimulate job growth even outside of the technology sector. Middle America soon found its buying power again.

"I see little commercial potential for the Internet for at least ten years."

—Bill Gates, 1994

Larry Page, born in 1973, inherited a natural ability with computers from both of his parents. At age six, Larry discovered computers and took a lasting interest in them.

Always creative, Page built an inkjet printer from Lego blocks as a computer engineering student at the University of Michigan. He graduated with honors and started a graduate program at Stanford University. There he met Sergey Brin, another graduate student with an interest in computer science. Together they designed a method for quickly finding information among the vast offering of Web pages. They wanted to improve upon existing search engines, which organized results by the number of times search terms appeared on a Web page. Their search engine organized pages by how many hits they received. The two creators figured the most popular pages were the most helpful to researchers, so they should be available first.

Page and Brin named their search engine Google after the math term *googol* (the number one followed by one hundred zeros), reflecting the abundance of information on the Web. At first, they were unable to find funding to launch their venture. Only a former Stanford PhD student who had cofounded Sun Microsystems recognized Google's potential. He handed them a check for one hundred thousand dollars in 1998. After the first investment, Page and

LARRY PAGE *(LEFT)* AND SERGEY BRIN *(RIGHT)* launched the Google search engine in the late 1990s to make surfing the Web easier.

Brin were able to raise one million dollars from other investors, friends, and family. Google, Inc., was born.

At first, the company headquarters was in a friend's garage in Menlo Park, California. Within a year, the company expanded to eight employees and larger office space in Palo Alto. The company fielded five hundred thousand queries a day, and showed no signs of slowing. *Google* was quickly adopted as a verb as people used the search engine to find their favorite celebrities, news topics, and their own names on the Internet.

By the end of the 1990s, Google became the most popular search engine worldwide. Into the next decade, Google upgraded its systems and devised new formats. In 2002 Page was honored as a Global Leader for Tomorrow by the World Economic Forum.

■ A RECORD SURPLUS

The economy of the late 1990s was in amazing shape compared to the beginning of the decade. Inflation, the rising price levels of goods and services, dipped to an annual rate of 1.6 percent in 1998, a thirty-three-year low. In 1999 the Dow Jones Industrial Average, the daily average of thirty major corporations' stock prices, soared to a new record high of 11,014.70. Both measures indicated that the U.S. economy was booming. Economists credited Clinton's policies. They also noted that the improvement might be due to cyclical trends (periodic reversals) in the economy.

Clinton had entered his first term of office with a $290 billion budget deficit. However, tax revenues grew as the economy improved over the next several years, shrinking the 1997 deficit to just $22 billion. That year Clinton worked with congressional Republicans to pass the Balanced Budget Act, a plan to eliminate the deficit entirely by 2002. Clinton agreed with Republicans that a balanced budget was important for the nation's future prosperity. After several more years of a soaring economy, he left office in 2001 with a $128 billion surplus, having generated a record surplus in 2000. Republican representative Bill Archer of Texas said, "This is a huge victory for American taxpayers and is the latest in a string of victories that Congress has won for our country and our economy."

Excited representatives of Cotelligent, Inc., celebrate with New York Stock Exchange chairman Richard Grasso *(center, with glasses)* at the **CLOSING OF THE STOCK MARKET ABOVE 11,000** on May 3, 1999.

Many OLDER AMERICANS in the 1990s chose to stay active.

CHAPTER FIVE

DECADE TRENDS:
PEOPLE, LIFESTYLES, ISSUES, AND EDUCATION

As historians evaluated the end of the century, they noticed certain trends. The average age of Americans had risen. Where families lived and how they worked, learned, and played had changed. Most newcomers to the United States settled in large urban areas. As immigrants filled inner-city neighborhoods, longtime residents continued their march to the suburbs. Housing complexes sprawled beyond city limits, sometimes hours from metropolitan downtowns. By 2000, 52 percent of the nation's population lived in suburbs. Those who were well off bought single-family homes and drove in ever larger, gas-guzzling sport-utility vehicles (SUVs).

■ GRAYING OF AMERICA

Between 1990 and 2000, the U.S. population rose by about 13 percent to 281.4 million people. The average age of Americans increased as well. Baby boomers born in the late 1940s, 1950s, and early 1960s had aged. As they grew older, the median age of the entire U.S. population jumped from 28 years in 1970 to 35.5 in 1999.

Better health care helped account for what some called the graying of America. Improvements in medicine permitted people to live longer. The new over-sixty-five crowd barely resembled their grandparents' generation. Overall, modern seniors felt better and were more active mentally and physically. Many stayed in their jobs longer or found other activities to keep them productive and occupied.

Another reason for the aging of America was declining birthrates. Broad use of birth control methods and better education about family planning, safe sex, and abstinence cut the rate of unplanned pregnancies. Abortion rates also dropped. The greatest decrease in unintended pregnancy occurred between 1990 and 1994 before leveling off. The rate decreased by one-quarter overall between 1990 and 2000.

■ WORKING WOMEN

American women continued to join the workforce in greater numbers. By 2000 half of all adult women worked. Women earned about seventy-six cents for every dollar a man made, a big improvement from previous decades. In 1983 women earned only about sixty-seven cents per male-earned dollar.

More women also achieved high-level positions than in earlier decades. One in three new doctors in 2000 was a woman, compared with four in one hundred in 1970. Women made up four in ten newly graduated lawyers in 2000. In 1970 that figure was fewer than one in ten. Women balanced the number of male graduates in almost every other profession, including dentists, businesspeople, and astronauts. After witnessing the treatment of Anita Hill during the Clarence Thomas hearings, women entered politics—and won offices—in the highest numbers yet.

A mother walks her son to school before heading to work herself. WOMEN WERE A STRONG PRESENCE IN MANY SECTORS OF THE 1990s WORKFORCE.

Career women tended to marry and have children later. In 2000, 22 percent of women ages thirty to thirty-four had not yet been married. A larger percentage of women than in the past never married at all. Those who did marry tended to have fewer children than women in previous decades.

By the end of the nineties, some married women tired of trying to manage what amounted to two full-time jobs: one at home and one at work. About 24 percent of husbands shared the housework load, and that number was increasing. But some couples who could afford to live on one salary did. Then the wife usually stayed home to raise children. However, one in ten married fathers whose wife worked stayed home with the children, another rising trend.

■ FAMILY ARRANGEMENTS

Into the 1990s, the traditional definition of family moved away from mom, dad, and kids. More adults of both genders lived on their own. Society grew more accepting of gay and lesbian couples openly living together. Increased numbers of couples divorced, delayed marriage, or never married. The number of children living with two parents dropped from 85 percent in 1970 to 65 percent in 2000. Similarly, the number of single moms swelled to 62 percent of single women. Although much

The picture of the American family expanded in the 1990s to include **GAY AND LESBIAN COUPLES WITH CHILDREN**. Here, Bill Dunn *(left)* and Shaun Morse sit with their three adopted boys, ages two, five, and six, on the porch of their Wichita, Kansas, home.

The McCaughey **SEPTUPLETS**, conceived through fertility treatment, celebrated their first birthday on November 8, 1998. They are the first septuplets to survive infancy.

smaller in number, dad-only households between 1970 and 1997 quadrupled, and their numbers kept growing. When neither parent could care for the children, grandparents assumed responsibility more commonly than in the past.

Delaying pregnancy sometimes contributed to more difficulty in becoming pregnant. Medical advances in fertility techniques helped women to have children even if they had been unable to become pregnant naturally. These treatments came with cause for concern, however. Modern techniques frequently resulted in multiple births. Between 1980 and 1998, the rate of triplet and higher numbers of multiple births rose by 400 percent. Going into the next century, twin birthrates doubled from 1980 numbers, climbing to 32.2 per 1,000 total births.

■ NEW IMMIGRANTS

New arrivals to the United States from Latin America, Asia, Europe, and Africa swelled the immigrant population. The number of foreign-born U.S. citizens rose from 17 million in 1990 to 28 million in 2000, the largest number ever.

Immigrants altered the balance among existing minority populations, such as African Americans. According to a report from the State University of New York at Albany, "In the 1990s, the number of blacks with recent roots in sub-Saharan Africa nearly tripled, while the number of blacks with origins in the Caribbean grew by more than 60 percent." In major cities such as New York and Boston, foreign-born black residents amounted to about 30 percent of the black population.

Mexicans made up the biggest share of legal immigrants to the United States. Typically, one hundred thousand Mexicans arrived each year. The Caribbean provided another large share of immigrants. Hundreds of thousands of immigrants from these countries also entered the United States illegally every year. Poverty and desperate conditions at home caused many without immigration papers to risk illegal entry in search of work and a better life.

Increased immigration caused some states to pull the welcome mat. "Critics charged that America was being 'overrun' with foreigners; they questioned whether Hispanics and Asians could be 'assimilated' into American culture," wrote historian George Tindall. Low-wage earners claimed immigrants took jobs they could use, even though these jobs often went unfilled without foreign-born workers. Residents of urban areas worried that use of social services by illegal immigrants drained local budgets.

Some California residents, in particular, complained about the rise in the state's Mexican population. Voters passed two controversial bills to limit rights of immigrants. The 1994 Proposition 187 prohibited illegal immigrants from receiving education, health care, and other public services. Four years later, voters supported legislation to end bilingual education in schools. However, both bills met with strong opposition from immigrant rights groups and other advocates. Although Proposition 187 passed, it was later ruled unconstitutional and was never implemented. As other states proposed similar bills in the following years, immigration became a hot topic nationwide.

In September 1994, protesters in Los Angeles, California, many of whom were immigrants, spoke out against the anti-immigration **PROPOSITION 187**.

A controversy concerning the right to die came to a head during the 1990s. For some patients who were close to death, extending life through extreme medical measures was unacceptable. They wanted to die peacefully and on their own terms. Increasingly, conservative religious groups and their supporters in government intervened. They believed it was a crime for doctors to withhold life-giving support.

Retired Michigan doctor Jack Kevorkian *(right)* brought the issue into the limelight. He thought doctors should have the right to help patients die painlessly. So he devised a suicide machine that ill patients could easily work themselves. The machine dispensed doses of a sleep-inducing drug followed by medication that would end life. Between 1990 and 1999, the man reporters called Dr. Death helped more than 130 people die.

Kevorkian's daring actions emboldened Oregon voters to pass the Death with Dignity Act in 1994. Oregon became the first U.S. state to legalize physician-assisted suicide for patients with less than six months to live. The law protected doctors who participated. While opponents fought the bill for ethical reasons, some also feared that sick adults would flock to Oregon to die. But after a few years of legal wrangling, the law was upheld.

In Michigan, however, state lawmakers hounded Kevorkian. The state passed a law against doctor-assisted suicide, hoping to pre-vent his work. State, town, and county lawyers tried to stop him in three costly trials. After each trial, the jury refused to convict him.

In 1998 Kevorkian publicized the issue in a new way. He helped a man with a deadly disease die while being filmed for CBS's *60 Minutes*. The film provided evidence for Michigan courts to find Kevorkian guilty of second-degree murder. The judge gave the seventy-seven-year-old ten to twenty-five years in prison. Kevorkian was released on parole in 2007. But his actions had succeeded in opening debate of the issue in a new light. After his sentencing, two states considered right-to-die laws similar to Oregon's. And larger numbers of older adults completed legal forms that required doctors to follow their directions for care and death, should they become gravely ill.

■ TOBACCO BATTLES

Another hot-button issue in the United States was nonsmokers' fight to breathe smoke-free air. Battles between smokers and nonsmokers had heated up throughout the 1980s. Reports publicized the dangers of smoking and the addictive nature of tobacco. By the 1990s, the federal government required that cigarette packages and advertisements carry warnings of health risks. Smoking on airplanes had been banned.

Even as more reports of illness from smoking and secondhand smoke emerged, industry heads denied the research. In a 1994 congressional hearing, seven leading tobacco company executives denied that their products were addictive or proven harmful. Jeffrey Wigand, a former tobacco-industry scientist and high-ranking executive, exposed the industry when he spoke out on CBS's *60 Minutes* in 1996. Wigand charged that the executives had lied under oath to Congress. His most damaging charges were that tobacco leaders knew they sold an addictive product because they added chemicals that intensified the addiction. Moreover, they knew these chemicals increased the risk of serious disease. According to Wigand, tobacco companies were in a "nicotine-delivery business," and the added chemicals were known as "impact boosting." The tobacco industry used these methods to hook new smokers quickly.

JEFFREY WIGAND *(left)* and attorney Ron Motley at a news conference in June 1997 after a settlement with the tobacco industry. Wigand later began an organization called Smoke-Free Kids. He wanted to counter the tobacco industry's strategy: "Hook them young and hook them for life."

Wigand's statements unleashed open war with the powerful tobacco industry. Some tobacco executives threatened CBS with a lawsuit to suppress the story. They organized a smear campaign to discredit Wigand and his story. Wigand received threats of physical harm to him and his family.

Wigand's brave stand resulted in new congressional investigations. His story encouraged others tobacco insiders to come forward. States began suing leading tobacco companies for knowingly causing health problems. In 1997 and 1998, the tobacco industry paid out billions of dollars in damages and agreed to fund nonsmoking programs.

■ RACIAL RIFTS AND RIOTS

Racial tensions in the United States were heightened early in the decade when a Los Angeles police incident gained national attention. On March 3, 1991, salesman George Holliday heard sirens outside his apartment. He grabbed his new video camera and, from his balcony, recorded four white Los Angeles Police Department (LAPD) officers beating African American motorist Rodney King. Police ordered King, who was behaving oddly, from his car and pounded him with fifty-six blows in eighty-one seconds. Outraged, Holliday offered his videotape to the media. Repeated broadcasts of the videotape confirmed many people's suspicion that Los Angeles police were prone to violence against blacks.

The four police were charged with using excessive force and suspended or fired from work. The video had been so heavily publicized that Judge Stanley

On March 3, 1991, a nearby witness videotaped this footage of the **BEATING OF RODNEY KING** by some officers of the Los Angeles Police Department.

In April 1992, **RIOTS BROKE OUT IN THE STREETS OF LOS ANGELES** following the acquittal of the officers accused of beating Rodney King.

Weisberg moved their trial to another county to get a fair hearing. On April 29, 1992, an all-white jury proclaimed the suspects not guilty. After hearing the police were free, Los Angeles mayor Tom Bradley and other black leaders condemned the verdict as a failure of the justice system.

Violence exploded in Los Angeles, beginning in black and Hispanic sections of the city. Rioting and looting spilled into the Koreatown neighborhood. Scared shopkeepers armed themselves. In an attempt to stop the violence, King himself pleaded on television, "Can we all get along?"

The National Guard, marines, and army soldiers were called in to restore order. By mid-May, the violence slowed to a trickle. After rioting ended, the city reported fifty-two people dead, six hundred buildings burned, and $900 million in property damage. The Los Angeles riots highlighted the racial divide that many thought had been bridged. Reporters called the violence and destruction "the worst incident of race rioting in American history." The nation was stunned.

■ "GO O. J."

Several years after the Rodney King beating, another televised event split the country between black and white. In June 1994, popular former Buffalo Bills football star and actor O. J. (Orenthal James) Simpson became a murder suspect five days after the grisly death of his wife, Nicole, and her friend, Ronald Goldman. As police approached Simpson's home, he fled in his Ford Bronco. Television cameras followed the sixty-five-minute high-speed police chase of Simpson's Bronco on the Los Angeles Freeway. Some viewers watched the spectacle on television, while others rushed to the freeway with signs saying, "Go O. J."

During his 1995 trial, **O. J. SIMPSON** tried on the bloody gloves from the murder of Simpson's ex-wife and her friend Ron Goldman. Simpson was found innocent in the criminal trial, but was later found guilty and fined $3.5 million in a civil trial brought by the families of Ron Goldman and Nicole Simpson.

Simpson eventually went to trial. As the story unfolded, media extensively covered the proceedings, and the country divided largely along racial lines. Many blacks believed Simpson was suspected unfairly, in part because he is African American. They pointed to the unequal treatment of different races often observed in law enforcement. Most whites found Simpson guilty due to his known history of physical abuse against his wife, who had just left him. For the trial, Simpson hired an expert (and expensive) team of defense lawyers. The trial dragged on for most of a year in court. On October 3, 1995, the jury found him not guilty.

Public reactions to the verdict were split. Most blacks celebrated, while the majority of whites were in disbelief. Race relations in the United States hit one of the lowest points since the 1960s.

■ SCHOOLS

A booming technology industry, factory closings, and jobs going overseas placed heavy demands on U.S. students. Without a good education, their ability to earn a living wage seemed increasingly bleak. The minimum hourly wage of $5.15 that Congress passed in 1997 was still not enough to raise a family. As a result of pressure and opportunity, young adults reached the highest levels of education yet. In 1998 more than 83 percent of GenXers had completed high school. Another 24 percent graduated from college, an all-time national high. Women accounted for more than half of these graduates.

Two weeks after Simpson's murder trial ended, Louis Farrakhan, head of the Nation of Islam religious organization, called out to African American men everywhere. He wanted them to take charge of their lives and change their image for the better. He organized a Million Man March on the National Mall in Washington, D.C., on October 16, 1995. An estimated 400,000 to 837,000 black men and boys gathered to answer Farrakhan's appeal to build a responsible black male community. Speakers from across the country urged participants to end drug use, gangs, violence, and unemployment.

The Million Man March received mixed reviews. Some reporters and women rejected the idea of a male-only gathering because it further divided races and genders, limiting women's roles. Angela Davis, an African American activist and professor at the University of California–Santa Cruz, concluded that "no march, movement, or agenda that defines manhood in the narrowest terms and seeks to make women lesser partners in this quest for equality can be considered a positive step."

But men and boys who attended the march felt energized. They came away with renewed self-respect and empowerment to make a difference. One man wrote: "I think we need to change the image of what people think we do. If we don't take charge to create and mold the perception that we want people to have of us, nobody else will."

75

In addition, more parents started their children's formal learning earlier. Enrollment in preschool for three- and four-year-olds increased from 50 to 58 percent between 1991 and 1999. Many others attended day care, where they received preparation for kindergarten.

The 1990s saw the issue of religion in public schools resurface. School prayer had been outlawed since mid-century as violating the separation of religion and government, a pillar of the U.S. Constitution. But some Americans wanted schools to start their day with a Christian prayer. They pushed supporters to run

"During the [Million Man] march . . . when somebody on the ground started singing, 'God Bless America, land that I love,' it really hit home that in an America where people can be treated equally, it really can be a land that you can love."

—*T. Dean Warner, lawyer and marcher, 1995*

for local school boards and advised people to sue school districts to allow prayers in public school. The question of prayer at extracurricular activities sponsored by public schools was a new variation on the issue in the 1990s. In 1999 a Houston, Texas, court ruled that student football players could not say student-led prayers while in huddles at games. The battle continued into the next century.

A different storm brewed over school vouchers. Some parents wanted money that the government spent on their child's public education to follow the child to whichever school the student attended. Parents of children in poorly performing schools liked the idea, as did those who wanted their children in religious schools, since the money in the form of vouchers could help them afford tuition there. But opponents saw vouchers as a way to have public money support children in religious schools, another violation of the separation of church and state.

■ YOUTH VIOLENCE

The decade saw an unnerving rise in school violence, ranging from robbery to assaults to gun violence. Drugs and gangs contributed to increased discipline problems, especially in secondary schools.

Some schools required uniforms as a way to promote discipline and equality. In 1994 the Long Beach Unified School District in California became the first city district to mandate uniforms. Two years later, in his second inaugural address, President Clinton noted improved behavior as a result of school uniforms, and the idea took hold. By the next school year, the number of students wearing uniforms jumped from a fraction of 1 percent to 3 percent. By 1999 principals of schools requiring uniforms reported a 91 percent reduction in overall crime, 90 percent drop in school suspensions, and 69 percent reduction in cases of vandalism.

No matter what changes educators made, however, school violence persisted. During the 1990s, gun violence erupted in eight different schools from Mississippi to Oregon. Between February 1996 and March 1999, an estimated fourteen school shootings occurred. Most were in small towns and middle-class neighborhoods. Murderers from ages eleven to sixteen killed fifteen classmates and teachers and wounded another forty-four.

Students console one another in the aftermath of the shooting at **COLUMBINE HIGH SCHOOL** in Colorado. On April 20, 1999, two students carrying guns entered the school, shooting students and teachers before killing themselves.

The most deadly incident involved two gun-wielding loners who attended Columbine High School in Littleton, Colorado. On April 20, 1999, the heavily armed pair, ages seventeen and eighteen, opened fire in the school. By the time the shooting stopped, the two teens had killed twelve students and one teacher and injured twenty-three others. Then they turned the guns on themselves. The boys had carefully planned the attack, modeling it on a video game. Another older boy had helped by buying the assault rifles at a gun show, where he faced no waiting period or background check.

The entire nation mourned the attack. Shocked, people wondered why two teens from seemingly good homes would create such horror. Experts cast blame on the ease of buying guns, violent video games and media, family problems, and social pressures. Communities rallied to make changes to prevent repeats. Schools launched programs to deal with bullied and loner children more effectively. Districts around the country installed metal detectors and began locker checks to keep weapons out of classes and hallways, efforts that were previously common only in some urban schools.

On the national level, Vice President Gore and his wife, Tipper, urged creation of V-chips—devices in new televisions that parents could use to block programs with excessive violence. President Clinton called for stricter laws for acquiring guns and background checks for buyers of guns. He requested more funding for violence prevention programs. Meanwhile, police across the country braced themselves for copycat shootings.

77

Author **TONI MORRISON** *[LEFT]* **ENJOYS A LAUGH WITH OPRAH WINFREY** on Winfrey's television talk show. Morrison's 1977 novel *Song of Solomon* was

CHAPTER SIX

THE WRITTEN WORD:
JOURNALISM, LITERATURE, AND MAGAZINES

Journalism and literature adapted in the 1990s as media expanded in the digital age. Boosted by the twenty-four-hour TV and Internet news cycle, star power in U.S. culture pervaded publishing and other media. Advertisements featuring celebrity endorsements skyrocketed. Photographers perched in trees overlooking private estates or hired cars and boats to follow the rich and famous for magazines and tabloid shows. To keep the public informed of entertainment industry news, the magazine *Entertainment Weekly* hit stands in 1990. The star-studded journal added to a long list of periodicals such as *People* that aimed to satisfy the public's appetite for celebrity gossip.

Publishers paid large amounts of money to stars who put their names on books and permitted interviews for magazine articles and other works. Some celebrities wrote polished pieces independently. Other times, ghostwriters wrote books for or with them. Publishers recognized that celebrity names sold products—in this case, the written word—no matter the quality.

One of the most notable examples of celebrity power was Oprah's Book Club. In 1996 Oprah launched the book club on a segment of her TV talk show, *The Oprah Winfrey Show*. Each month she highlighted a book that she recommended. She interviewed the author and often featured segments related to the book's theme. Oprah's reading selections flew off bookstore shelves and made instant hits of the books and authors. The rise in sales for titles in Oprah's Book Club has become known as the Oprah effect. One benefit of Oprah's Book Club is that readership multiplies—thanks in part to her celebrity endorsements.

■ BUYING AND READING BOOKS ONLINE

People bought books in new places and new ways in the 1990s. Big-box stores such as Wal-Mart offered books at reduced prices, stealing sales from even the largest bookstore chains. But the decade experienced the most rapid book sale expansion from online booksellers and publishers, particularly Amazon.com. From its start in 1995, this online retailer aimed to provide customers with books at low prices. Often it even shipped orders free of charge. Jeff Bezos, the company's founder, made customer service a priority at Amazon and earned returning customers at an astounding rate.

> **" Other booksellers will do what they have to do [to compete with Amazon.com]; there's too much risk in not being on the Internet."**
>
> —*Robert Natale, director of equity research at Standard & Poor's (a publisher of financial research and analysis), 1997*

JEFF BEZOS is the creator of Amazon.com, where customers can order books online and receive their orders through the mail. Bezos was named *Time* magazine's Person of the Year in 1999. *Time* editors choose the person they think has had the most influence during any given year.

JOHN GRISHAM signs autographs in April 1996 at the University of Mississippi.

Amazon's success pushed bookstore chains such as Barnes & Noble and Borders to sell online too. Small booksellers found themselves competing against discount prices at large retailers and convenient online companies with huge warehouse collections. Many small stores folded, unable to survive in the changing market. The trend toward online book buying skyrocketed by the end of the nineties.

By the end of the decade, publishers also saw the potential of e-books. Several companies began offering electronic versions of current, copyrighted books that customers could purchase and download. Some companies worked with libraries to provide patrons with access to e-books, extending the libraries' collections. However, going into the new millennium, most people continued to prefer reading books in their traditional, print format.

■ POPULAR READS

John Grisham led the pack of popular authors with his best-selling thrillers. During the 1990s, he held five of the top ten slots on the *New York Times* bestseller list, with sales of about 60 million books. Readers particularly liked *The Firm* (1991), *The Pelican Brief* (1992), *The Chamber* (1994), and *The Testament* (1999). Stephen King came in second in sales, releasing new horror titles including *Dolores Claiborne* (1993), *The Green Mile* (1996), and *Bag of Bones* (1998). Titles from both authors were made into popular movies. Michael Crichton also scored doubly with several books that eventually became big-screen hits. Crichton sold millions of the science fiction thrillers *Jurassic Park* (1990), *The Lost World* (1995), and *Twister* (1996).

Danielle Steel regularly found her dramatic and romantic novels on bestseller lists. She began writing in the 1970s and took off in the eighties and

Barbara Kingsolver emerged as one of the decade's notable authors through books written from her varied life experiences. Born in 1955, she lived in many places while growing up, including Africa and Kentucky. She enjoyed writing poems and stories and was first published as a child, when an essay she had written was printed in the local paper.

Always curious, Kingsolver switched college majors at DePauw University in Greencastle, Indiana, from music to biology and also studied writing. After she graduated, Kingsolver lived in Greece, France, and the United Kingdom. She eventually settled in Tucson, Arizona. A variety of odd jobs helped her pay her way through a graduate program in biology at the University of Arizona. Each place and job provided interesting tidbits for future nonfiction books, novels, and short stories.

Kingsolver's first novel, *The Bean Trees*, appeared in 1988. Drawing on her familiarity with the southern and southwestern U.S. landscape and culture, it received modest acclaim at first. But as she published more works that earned praise, this first title gained a following. High school and college literature courses added *The Bean Trees* to their curriculum, and the book was translated into more than ten languages.

During the 1990s, Kingsolver published five acclaimed fiction and nonfiction books that recalled different aspects of her life. *Pigs in Heaven* (1993), the sequel to *The Bean Trees*, won recognition for Kingsolver's "extravagantly gifted narrative voice." *The Poisonwood Bible* (1998) followed a missionary family in the Congo and won the National Book Prize of South Africa. It was a finalist for the Pulitzer Prize and earned publicity as part of Oprah's Book Club. President Bill Clinton awarded Kingsolver the National Humanities Medal in 2000. Since then she has added novels and essays to her list of works. In 2007 she recounted her family's yearlong experiment in eating locally grown food in *Animal, Vegetable, Miracle*. She continues to be a distinguished author of the twenty-first century.

nineties with such titles as *Mixed Blessings* (1992), *Lightning* (1995), and *The Long Road Home* (1998). Each sold millions of copies.

Several literary novels gained attention during the decade. Amy Tan's *The Kitchen God's Wife* (1991) and Charles Frazier's *Cold Mountain* (1997) earned prizes and readers. Barbara Kingsolver's acclaimed novel *The Poisonwood Bible*

(1998) won extra recognition when it was selected for Oprah's Book Club in 2000. Toni Morrison published her sixth novel, *Jazz*, in 1992, and was awarded the 1993 Nobel Prize in Literature for her numerous novels and essays. *Beloved*, Morrison's Pulitzer Prize–winning novel about the horrors of slavery, was adapted to film in 1998. Oprah Winfrey produced and starred in the movie.

Jack Canfield and Mark Victor Hansen stole the nonfiction market with their popular Chicken Soup for the Soul series. Their first collection of 101 inspirational stories came out in 1993. By 1998 the two authors had seven titles on the best-seller list. A different guide to relationships, John Gray's *Men Are from Mars, Women Are from Venus* (1992), explored gender and romance and sold 6.6 million copies by 1999. Diet books remained another mainstay of popular nonfiction books. Two standouts were Barry Sears's *The Zone* (1995) and *Dr. Atkins' New Diet Revolution* (1999) from Robert C. Atkins. Americans flocked to buy these guides to new weight-loss philosophies.

■ FOR YOUNGER READERS

Young readers devoured books that transported them to different places and times. A few series of the nineties stood out for their creativity, solid writing, and ability to hold readers' attention.

R. L. Stine brought mystery and horror to kid's books. His first series, Fear Street, began in 1989 and quickly became a hot seller for young adults. Since the first Fear Street title, Stine has published more than one hundred books in the series. Stine's Goosebumps series for

R. L. STINE checks out masks for the *Goosebumps* TV series. The TV show debuted in 1995 and was based on Stine's popular set of children's horror books.

Each year, the American Library Association awards the Newbery Medal to an author of the most distinguished new book for children. The following titles won the Newbery Award in the 1990s.

1990 *Number the Stars*, Lois Lowry
1991 *Maniac Magee*, Jerry Spinelli
1992 *Shiloh*, Phyllis Reynolds Naylor
1993 *Missing May*, Cynthia Rylant
1994 *The Giver*, Lois Lowry
1995 *Walk Two Moons*, Sharon Creech
1996 *The Midwife's Apprentice*, Karen Cushman
1997 *The View from Saturday*, E. L. Konigsburg
1998 *Out of the Dust*, Karen Hesse
1999 *Holes*, Louis Sachar

middle schoolers debuted in 1992. This series catapulted Stine to celebrity status, with books translated into thirty-two languages and into a must-watch television show that appeared in the mid-nineties. Stine was happy to meet the demand for new books. He mused, "My job is to make kids laugh and give them the CREEPS!"

Despite the popularity of Stine's books, nothing compared to the phenomenon of J. K. Rowling's fantasy series about a wizard in training, Harry Potter. In 1997 British publisher Bloomsbury released one thousand copies of *Harry Potter and the Philosopher's*

J. K. ROWLING signs books for Harry Potter fans in October 1999.

Stone. Scholastic produced the U.S. version, retitled *Harry Potter and the Sorcerer's Stone*, in 1998, and the book leaped onto U.S. best-seller lists by the end of the year. Adults as well as children were drawn into Harry's magical adventures at the Hogwarts School of Witchcraft and Wizardry. Soon *Harry Potter and the Chamber of Secrets* hit bookstores, and in 1999, readers clamored for the third novel, *Harry Potter and the Prisoner of Azkaban*.

By then the books had earned a series of awards, and each new release became a major hit. Harry Potter mania had swept the country. Booksellers held opening parties with long lines of buyers. Children too young to read the books begged their parents to read them aloud. Reading became a major family event in response to Rowling's books. A new classic had been born.

■ BOOK BANNING

The Harry Potter books as well as a number of older classics came under fire as book banning gained momentum in the 1990s. Those who opposed the themes of certain books and wanted the books eliminated from school and library collections found support. Favorite titles such as *The Adventures of Huckleberry Finn* by Mark Twain, *Blubber* by Judy Blume, *Bridge to Terabithia* by Katherine Paterson, and countless other books became controversial choices in some neighborhoods.

Proponents of book banning often focused on titles they claimed encouraged witchcraft, including *The Witches* by Roald Dahl, *Scary Stories to Tell in the Dark* by Alvin Schwartz, and the Harry Potter books. They also targeted books with racial or sexual themes, especially those featuring families with same-sex couples. However, in most places, librarians and many others successfully opposed these restrictions.

Models walk the catwalk in a 1997 fashion show in Paris, France. The "HEROIN CHIC" trend, characterized by gaunt faces and bodies, dark eyes, and pale skin, took off in fashion capitals such as Paris and New York.

CHAPTER SEVEN

SEEING IS BELIEVING:
FADS, FASHION, AND VISUAL ARTS IN THE 1990s

Trends in the early 1990s turned away from the showy mass consuming that highlighted the 1980s. Fashions were more understated, and artists and architecture displayed simpler lines. But a disconnect arose between trends that tilted toward the natural and unadorned and advertising's fashion emphasis on looking like a model. As the economy rebounded later in the decade, fashion reflected a new wave of consumerism that would carry into the new millennium.

■ IMPOSSIBLY THIN MODELS

The obsession with women's weight and being thin reached new heights during the 1990s. At the beginning of the decade, the average female model fit into size 6 clothing, the size of samples from designers. By the close of the decade, samples had shrunk to size 2, and so did the models. Although the U.S. population was growing more overweight, advertisements often featured gaunt, stick-thin young women and men.

This trend is often attributed to a 1992 Calvin Klein ad campaign featuring young British model Kate Moss. Moss was not as tall or curvy as other supermodels of the time. Her look—the waif look, as it was called—spawned a wave of advertising featuring extremely skinny models wearing little makeup and plain, casual clothing. In addition,

KATE MOSS models a dress by designer Calvin Klein at a 1998 New York fashion show.

fashion associated with grunge music of the early nineties went mainstream, bringing the "heroin chic" trend to runways by the middle of the decade. The trend's name came from models' accentuated gaunt features, messy hair, and sweaty look that resembled those of heroin addicts. While clothing styles changed from season to season, the skinnier standard for models had staying power.

Young girls saw increasingly thinner models and actresses on magazine covers, in movies, and on TV. Concerned parents and others criticized the fashion industry and culture for creating unrealistic standards. Eating disorders such as anorexia nervosa and bulimia gained national attention as growing numbers of young women and some men tried to achieve impossibly thin bodies.

■ FASHION FADS

The 1980s trends had featured flashy, expensive fashions. Nineties shoppers of all ages wanted simpler clothes. From businesses to classrooms, Americans chose comfortable, casual clothes. Polar fleece vests, jackets, pants, socks, and gloves became popular casual attire. In addition, sporty outfits once reserved for workouts became common street clothes. Comfy athletic shoes and nylon and polyester wind pants designed to insulate joggers from the wind became indoor and outdoor everyday wear.

Casual dress replaced formal suits and ties for men and dresses and high heels for women in many workplaces. From the beginning of the decade until the end, the number of companies that allowed casual dress days jumped from 7 percent to 53 percent. As a result, casual work clothes became big business. Designers scrambled to create lines that suited relaxed work environments. Shoulder pads, popular in the eighties, softened or disappeared from shirts and jackets. New soft materials, such as Tencel and microfiber, hung in relaxed shapes. And women professionals began to wear pants as well as skirts and dresses—a departure from workplace dress codes of previous decades.

■ MAKING A STATEMENT

Fashion of the nineties showed a person's identity and individuality. Preppy clothes resembling golf club attire were popular with professionals who wanted to sport a business casual look. Men wore sports jackets or cotton shirts with beige or navy slacks or chinos. Women wore a similar version of pants and a tailored blouse. Many took their fashion cues from popular TV sitcoms. Fans of the character Rachel on *Friends*, played by Jennifer Aniston, copied her tailored, fashionable style.

Not everyone liked the preppy look. Hip-hop musicians wore leather and flashy colors, extremely baggy jeans, sports jerseys or sweatshirts, and expensive athletic shoes. By the mid-1990s, the punk and goth looks of the previous decade had been revived among teenagers. Fans copied bands such as Nine Inch Nails and Marilyn Manson, who wore all-black outfits, often with studs and spikes. (The name "goth" came from dressing in black, like dark characters in gothic novels set in medieval castles or Victorian times.)

Fans of the **GOTH** band the Creatures wear goth makeup, piercings, and clothing.

Chris Cornell of Soundgarden performs at the Lollapalooza music festival in 1992. Soundgarden was formed in Seattle, the capital of the grunge music scene. **GRUNGE FASHION** was based on the antifashion style of many Seattle musicians in the late 1980s and early 1990s.

Followers of grunge wanted nothing of these showy looks. Instead, they preferred to look anti any style. Young men grew their hair long and greasy to counter the clean-cut yuppie or Mohawked punk images. Both genders donned baggy and torn cargo pants, jeans, or overalls. They wore oversized flannel shirts over T-shirts. This trend eventually earned its own place in the fashion market. Designers such as Calvin Klein and the clothing chain Abercrombie & Fitch picked up on the style. They sold ripped jeans and cardigan sweaters at high-fashion prices. Chunky Doc Martens boots, Birkenstock sandals, and casual shoes from Converse and Vans were also a popular part of the grunge look, despite their often high prices.

As the decade continued, other fads emerged. Styles from the 1960s and 1970s enjoyed a revival, including tie-dye with bright yellows, oranges, and pinks replacing the overwhelmingly black, dark brown, olive green, and beige items. Bell-bottoms of the early to mid nineties later gave way to wide-leg jeans (wider throughout the leg instead of just below the knee). Near the end

> # "Fashion is getting more primitive. [Piercing] is just part of an antifashion period."

—Zandra Rhodes, designer, on the appearance of body piercings on fashion runways, 1993

of the 1990s, slightly flared bootleg jeans hung loosely over boots, sandals, or name-brand athletic shoes.

■ ACCESSORIZING

Big hair from the 1980s relaxed into sleeker or sporty chopped hairdos. Many women copied the shoulder-length, choppy layered hairstyles of celebrities such as actresses Jennifer Aniston and Meg Ryan. Goth teens dyed their hair black and cut it into short, punky hairdos. They wore dark makeup, black nail polish, and metal chains for accessories. Most teens, however, went for less obvious adornment, such as glitter for their cheeks, eyelids, or hair.

Piercings and tattoos became popular as a mode of personal expression or marks of individuality. Teens pierced their tongues, belly buttons, eyebrows, noses, ears, nipples, or a combination of these. Rock stars and even pop stars such as the Spice Girls sported tattoos. Tattoos and piercings no longer carried a tough-guy or biker image, as they once had. They became accepted adornment, at least among teens and GenXers.

91

JENNIFER ANISTON of the TV show *Friends* sported a layered hairstyle she made popular in the 1990s.

Madonna gained fame during the 1980s for her unique style, open sexuality, rebellious attitude, and infectious music. Bright and intensely ambitious, Madonna Louise Veronica Ciccone was driven to achieve after losing her mother at a young age and enduring a turbulent homelife with her stepmother. Once her music career took off in the early eighties, her teenage rebellion against her strict Catholic upbringing revealed itself. She sported fishnet stockings, fingerless gloves, lace bra tops, and crucifix necklaces. Concerts and videos exhibited images of burning crosses, sex, and religion.

Into the 1990s, Madonna continued to push cultural boundaries. In 1990 the pope called for a ban on her sexually charged performances, such as one in a cone-shaped bra designed by Jean-Paul Gaultier, in the Blond Ambition World Tour *(above right)*. She responded by releasing a greatest hits album called *The Immaculate Collection*, a play on the Catholic belief in the Immaculate Conception. (This belief says that Mary, the mother of Jesus— also called the Madonna—was born without sin.) In 1992 Madonna founded Maverick Records, her own record company, with Time Warner. By then a movie actress, songwriter, dancer, and businesswoman, she added publication of the book *Sex* to her achievements that year, along with the release of her album *Erotica*. The 1993 world tour supporting the album featured Madonna in costumes as varied as military gear, wigs and headdresses,

a tuxedo, and Victorian dresses. Later in the decade, she sported a sleeker look and scored hits with the album *Ray of Light* (1998) and the song "Beautiful Stranger" for the soundtrack of the 1999 movie *Austin Powers: The Spy Who Shagged Me*. With each reinvention of her look and sound, Madonna was known for her shock factor.

Throughout the nineties, fans continued to look to Madonna for edgy fashion. From dominatrix to old-school glamour to updated and toned-down casual, her style remained media worthy. In 1998 she was named Most Fashionable Artist (female) at the VH1/Vogue Fashion Awards. She eventually broadened her fashion appeal by designing a clothing line for European retailer H&M. By the twenty-first century, she had become one of the top earning stars of all time.

■ ART ALIVE, DIGITAL, AND REDEFINED

Art in the 1990s branched out along different paths. Performance art, in which humans interact with other art forms in a brief live performance, gained admittance into art museums. Exhibits blended any combination of video, paintings, sculpture, and photography with human antics into one installation. The idea was for viewers to come away with a total experience, one more emotional than seeing a single visual image. Topics were in-your-face. Artists depicted sex, violence, and gender differences to spur reactions from viewers.

A new addition to the art world was digital art. Technology in the 1990s gave artists unlimited potential for expression. Because computer software was not affordable for most artists, corporations gave money to artists to create visuals with their programs. Digital art went mainstream to collectors in the art world after the Whitney Museum in New York City featured digital art in an exhibit in 1997. Two years later, the Whitney announced another show of digital art, from interactive websites to other multimedia formats.

■ BUILDING MUSEUMS AND SKYSCRAPERS

During the 1990s, U.S. architects generally broke from the glitzy design style of the eighties. Richard Meier designed the curving Getty Center in Los Angeles, a center for art displays and education completed in 1997. It includes the J. Paul Getty Museum, a 450-seat auditorium, and gardens on 110 acres (45 hectares) of a hill overlooking the city and the ocean. The center earned Meier the American Institute of Architecture's highest honor, the AIA Gold Medal.

THE GETTY CENTER in Los Angeles, California, was completed in 1997.

Martha Stewart was the queen of stylish living in the 1990s. She was born to middle-class parents in 1941 and was always hard-working. Martha enjoyed learning about orderly gardening, cooking, canning, and sewing. At Barnard College in New York City, she worked as a model to help pay bills. Martha married Andrew Stewart, then finished her degree and later joined her father-in-law as a stockbroker. This experience gave her business training she would put to good use.

Stewart and her family moved to Westport, Connecticut, in 1973. After renovating their house, she started a catering business from her basement, creating a $1 million company within ten years. Meanwhile, Stewart wrote articles about home decorating and gourmet cooking for the *New York Times* and the magazine *House Beautiful*.

In 1982 she turned these articles into the book *Entertaining*. The book made her a household name and earned her regular appearances on the TV talk show *Today*. The appearances led to a $5 million contract with Kmart to design a line of products.

While her career was charging ahead, Stewart's marriage was falling apart. In 1987 Andy moved out of their house. He was having an affair with one of Martha's assistants. As rumors about the cause of the split flew through the media, fans read reports of Martha's controlling and arrogant

MARTHA STEWART poses in the kitchen facility at her television studio in 1998. She filmed *Martha Stewart Living* there.

tendencies. This Martha was very different from the perfect housewife she portrayed on television. The couple divorced in 1990. Martha coped by keeping busy with work.

Following the success of her television show *Martha Stewart Living*, Stewart signed a high-paying new contract with Kmart in 1997. She used that income to create her one-woman multimedia giant corporation, Martha Stewart Living Omnimedia, Inc. According to Stewart, "I am a maniacal perfectionist. And if I weren't, I wouldn't have this company."

Stewart's perfectionist ways to maintain a home offended some who felt she was too old-fashioned. But she inspired people too. Many looked to Stewart for ideas. Even after serving time in prison in 2004 for stock fraud, Martha has come back strong with *The Martha Stewart Show*, its companion website, and a catalog company called Martha by Mail selling her own product line.

In 1990 downtown Chicago added Two Prudential Plaza to its landscape of award-winning buildings. At its completion, the 995-foot (303-meter) tower was the fifth highest in Chicago and the tallest reinforced concrete building in North America. The skyscraper is distinguished among the Chicago skyline by its stepped-back chevron (arrow-shaped) sides, centered glass columns, diamond-shaped top, and 80-foot (24 m) spire.

Between Fifth and Madison avenues in New York, the LVMH Tower, completed in 1999, stands out against its neighbors on East 57th Street. The North American headquarters of luxury goods company Louis Vuitton was designed by the French architect Christian de Portzamparc. Set on a narrow plot of Manhattan property, the geometric and curving lines of the tower's glass walls helped to maximize space in its twenty-three stories.

■ INSIDE HOMES

As architects designed imaginative buildings, other influences affected what furnishings and decoration looked like inside. Feng shui, meaning "wind-water" in Chinese, was gaining attention in the United States. This is the ancient Chinese plan for positioning objects in a way that improves chi (qi), or energy flows. Traditionally, this was believed to improve the lives of those who occupied the planned spaces. Designers and landscape architects introduced feng shui principles to U.S. consumers during the 1990s. These principles became popular in arranging rooms, gardens, and placement of rooms added to houses. Books on the subject helped guide individuals in placing their furniture and knickknacks.

Bernard Shaw
CNN Reporting

■ Bagh
Iraq

CNN correspondent Bernard Shaw described, via satellite phone, the
BOMBING OF BAGHDAD, IRAQ, on January 16, 1991. He was one of
three CNN reporters who brought viewers twenty-four-hour coverage of
the Persian Gulf War.

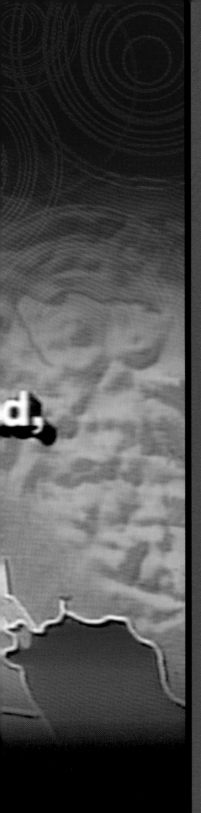

CHAPTER EIGHT

FRIENDS, FAMILIES, AND REALITY:

TELEVISION, MOVIES, AND THEATER

New technology spawned a rise in the number of television stations available to viewers. Cable networks offered an array of stations for a monthly fee. Some stations devoted programming to specific genres, such as sports, news, children's shows, comedy, or music videos. Regular television stations scrambled for concepts that would keep viewers watching their shows.

CHANGING MEDIA AND NEWS

High-tech media brought the Persian Gulf War to home viewers in a different way from previous conflicts. Cable News Network (CNN), a twenty-four-hour network launched in 1980, expanded in the nineties into Japan, Europe, Asia, and the Middle East. After U.S. bombs destroyed electricity and telephone in Iraq's capital, Baghdad, only CNN's private copper phone lines and satellite transmission worked. Once bombing started, the three main U.S. television networks, ABC, NBC, and CBS, pulled their reporters from Iraq. But Saddam Hussein allowed CNN reporters to remain in Baghdad without threat of harm. He saw their international reach as a way to broadcast his message around the world.

Reporters Peter Arnett, John Holliman, and Bernard Shaw provided the first live coverage of war. CNN's twenty-four-hour coverage attracted the attention of viewers at home and quickly earned the growing network ratings that compared

George Clooney's career began when his newscaster and talk show host father brought him onstage. Born in 1961, he was nurtured in show business by his dad, his beauty-pageant mother, and his aunt, famous singer Rosemary Clooney. In 1982 Clooney moved to Los Angeles. After a few years of rough starts, he landed bit parts on shows such as *Roseanne* and *The Golden Girls*.

Clooney drew attention after landing the role of handsome doctor Doug Ross in the popular television series *ER* (begun in 1994). From then on, he caused sensations wherever he went with his drop-dead good looks. His acting skills earned praise too, winning him an Emmy Award for his role on *ER*. Television successes led to roles in movies, such as the romantic comedy *One Fine Day* (1996), *Batman and Robin* (1997), and the military movie *Three Kings* (1999).

GEORGE CLOONEY *(above in 1997)* was born in Kentucky and made a splash in Hollywood.

Clooney balanced his career with projects that sent humanitarian political messages. He went on to become a respected producer, director, and screenwriter. But his image as a hunk attracted the most attention. In 1997 and again in 2006, *People* magazine named Clooney the "Sexiest Man Alive." The magazine justified their selection with the pronouncement, "*People*'s choice cut of beef is heartstoppingly handsome, funny, and—catch this—nice, too."

with the big three. High ratings lasted throughout the war as more viewers hungry for on-the-spot reporting discovered CNN. "When there was a disaster, it used to be that people went to church and all held hands. . . . Now the minute anything happens, they all run to CNN and think, 'The whole world is sharing this experience with me,'" said Don Hewitt, producer of CBS's *60 Minutes*.

■ TELEVISION SITCOMS WITH A KICK

Situation comedies about families, such as *Growing Pains*, *Full House*, and *The Fresh Prince of Bel-Air*, attracted sizable audiences during the 1990s. In 1990

Seinfeld made entertainment out of everyday situations faced by a group of quirky single friends. This sitcom starred the show's namesake, comedian Jerry Seinfeld, and proclaimed itself a "show about nothing." *Friends*, which debuted in 1994, followed the lives of three men and three women. Both shows became wildly popular.

Several young-adult series blended family story lines with teenage or twenty-something drama. *Melrose Place* and *Beverly Hills, 90210* revolved around wealthy, often spoiled teens and young adults. *My So-Called Life*, *Party of Five*, and *Dawson's Creek* featured middle-class teens. These shows dealt with edgy topics such as drug use, partner abuse, censorship, and homelessness.

Gays and lesbians took center stage for the first time on television. The popular sitcom *Ellen*, starring Ellen DeGeneres, ran from 1994 until 1998. In a 1997 episode, the main character outed herself as a lesbian. The episode aired two weeks after DeGeneres herself had come out on the cover of *Time* magazine. Her character became the first sitcom star to announce her sexual orientation on television. In 1998 *Will & Grace* appeared. This sitcom featured a gay lawyer, Will, living with his female best friend, Grace, a straight interior designer. The show ran for eight years, earned sixteen Emmy Awards, and made stars of Debra Messing, Eric McCormack, Sean Hayes, and Megan Mullally.

99

Ellen DeGeneres *(seated center)* with the cast of **ELLEN** in 1997. Ellen was TV's first out lesbian.

Marge, Maggie, Lisa, Bart, and Homer Simpson made their animated sitcom debut in December 1989. *THE SIMPSONS* was such a success that *The Simpsons Movie (above)* hit theaters in 2007.

■ PRIME-TIME CARTOONS

At one time, television networks claimed animated shows would never attract viewers during prime time. They were expensive to produce, too juvenile, and could never tackle serious material. That view changed with the introduction of *The Simpsons*. Cartoon shorts of *The Simpsons*, created for a general audience instead of children, had appeared between segments of the *Tracey Ullman Show* during the 1980s. The shorts proved so popular that *The Simpsons* became an independent show on Fox, still a young network in 1990. The instant cartoon hit allowed Fox to compete with the main networks for the first time.

Soon other adult-oriented animated shows were added, such as *Beavis & Butt-Head* (MTV, 1993), *South Park* (Comedy Central, 1997), and *King of the Hill* (Fox, 1997). All had irreverent characters who made fun of everything from religion to politics to strange parents. Critics opposed the foul language and bathroom humor, but viewers loved the shows. In 1997 *The Simpsons* became the longest-running prime-time animated series.

■ REALITY TV

Networks liked the idea of reality TV. Following regular people around with a camera was a cheap mode of production, and reality shows didn't require paying star salaries. *COPS*, premiering in 1989, tracked police on duty and was the first reality show to interest viewers in the early 1990s. MTV's *The Real World* began in 1992. The show thrust seven strangers into an unscripted living situation for several months and recorded their interactions. The edited

Popular movies of the 1990s offered a mix of topics and actors. The following movies earned Academy Awards as the year's best film:

1990 *Dances with Wolves*, starring Kevin Costner

1991 *Silence of the Lambs*, starring Jodie Foster and Anthony Hopkins

1992 *Unforgiven*, starring Clint Eastwood, Morgan Freeman, and Gene Hackman

1993 *Schindler's List*, starring Liam Neeson and Ben Kingsley

1994 *Forrest Gump*, starring Tom Hanks and Robin Wright Penn

1995 *Braveheart*, starring Mel Gibson

1996 *The English Patient*, starring Ralph Fiennes and Kristin Scott Thomas

1997 *Titanic*, starring Kate Winslet and Leonardo DiCaprio

1998 *Shakespeare in Love*, starring Gwyneth Paltrow, Joseph Fiennes, and Geoffrey Rush

1999 *American Beauty*, starring Kevin Spacey and Annette Bening

101

twenty-two-minute episodes highlighted conflicts and dramatic moments. *The Real World* became so popular that *Saturday Night Live*, a live TV comedy show, spoofed it in a 1993 sketch. MTV followed with the road-trip reality show *Road Rules* in 1995, another hit. The popularity of this concept paved the way for the boom of reality shows that came in the early twenty-first century.

■ THE BIG SCREEN

The 1990s was a good decade for movies of every genre. Directors took on serious historical events in dramas, including African American activism in *Malcolm X* (1992), the Holocaust in *Schindler's List* (1993), the slave trade in *Amistad* (1997), and World War II in *Saving Private Ryan* (1998). Romantic comedies abounded, ranging from the classic romance *Sleepless in Seattle* (1993) to the quirky *10 Things I Hate About You* (1999). Advancements in technology made for films with impressive special effects. *Jurassic Park* (1993), *Independence Day* (1996), *Men in Black* (1997), and *Titanic* (1997) wowed audiences with larger-than-life effects that were more realistic than ever. And in 1995, *Toy Story*, the first full-length computer-animated movie, won over audiences as the animation of the future.

Many movies of the decade initiated careers. In 1990 *Home Alone* made child actor Macauley Culkin—outwitting robbers after his family accidentally leaves on vacation without him—an instant star. The same year, Julia Roberts played a prostitute who goes from rags to riches in *Pretty Woman*, gaining fame for her mile-wide smile. Tom Hanks became a leading man of the decade with a wide range of roles. He showed his versatility as a lawyer dying of AIDS in *Philadelphia* (1993), the simple-minded hero of *Forrest Gump* (1994), and an astronaut in *Apollo 13* (1995). The 1997 film *Good Will Hunting* also introduced Matt Damon and Ben Affleck as actors and screenwriters, earning them an Oscar for their writing talent. One of the most popular movies of the decade, *Titanic* (1997), launched Leonardo

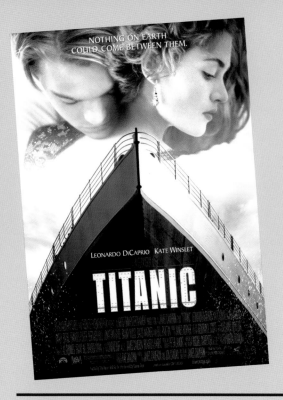

Kate Winslet and Leonardo DiCaprio starred in the megahit *TITANIC* in 1997. At the time, it was the most expensive movie ever made and the highest-grossing movie at the box office.

DiCaprio and Kate Winslet into superstardom as lovers on the sinking ship. The film won eleven Academy Awards including Best Picture and quickly became the highest-earning movie of all time. Its theme song, "My Heart Will Go On," dominated radio airwaves and became the signature song of singer Celine Dion.

Several television comedians turned to film acting. Adam Sandler starred in *Happy Gilmore* (1996) and *The Wedding Singer* (1998), showing off sensitive and comic acting skills. Mike Meyers scored hits with his *Austin Powers* movies in 1997 and 1999, portraying a 1960s hipster secret agent unfrozen in the 1990s to battle Dr. Evil. And Will Smith of TV's *The Fresh Prince of Bel-Air* launched a career as an action-film hero beginning with 1996's *Independence Day*.

■ THEATER

Theater took chances by bringing new styles and sounds to Broadway. Walt Disney Studios turned two of its animated movies into stage productions.

❝You can't have a great love story without death being a factor.❞

—*James Cameron, director of* Titanic, *1997*

Beauty and the Beast (1994) and *The Lion King* (1998), featuring music by Elton John, appealed to families who were not usually theatergoers. They became huge hits.

Nineties stage shows, like television, attacked edgier topics. First performed in 1990 in Los Angeles, Tony Kushner's *Angels in America* broke new ground featuring AIDS and gay relationships as the main themes. The epic two-part story stretched over seven hours. The award-winning show gained fame internationally and was adapted to an HBO miniseries in 2003 as well as an opera in 2004.

The rock musical *Rent*, based on the 1896 opera *La Bohème* by Giacomo Puccini, gained considerable attention in 1996 as a youthful sound on Broadway. *Rent* tracked a year in the life of young artists and musicians in New York, addressing HIV/AIDS, homelessness, and drugs. The musical drew mobs of repeat followers for its modern sound, honesty, and touching exposure of the disease. The show's creator, Jonathan Larson, never knew its success—he died suddenly the night of the final dress rehearsal. But the award-winning musical continued around the world into the next decade, becoming a movie in 2005 and running on Broadway until 2008.

Tap dancing returned to the stage in 1996 with *Bring in 'da Noise/Bring in 'da Funk*, starring twenty-three-year-old Savion Glover. The young king of tap soared across the stage, earning a Tony award for best choreography. Glover had spent five years dancing on the TV show *Sesame Street* (1990–1995), and this musical made him a household name. After the show, Glover was featured on TV, with singer Barbra Streisand in her *Timeless* 1999 live concert, and in Spike Lee's 2000 film *Bamboozled*.

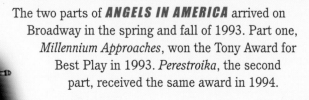

The two parts of **ANGELS IN AMERICA** arrived on Broadway in the spring and fall of 1993. Part one, *Millennium Approaches*, won the Tony Award for Best Play in 1993. *Perestroika*, the second part, received the same award in 1994.

SNOOP DOGGY DOGG rocks a crowd at the Lollapalooza
music festival in 1997. In addition to his music career, Snoop
Dogg (born Cordozar Calvin Broadus Jr.) has made dozens of
appearances in films and on television.

CHAPTER NINE

FROM GRUNGE TO THE MACARENA:
MUSIC AND DANCE OF THE 1990s

With MTV in its second decade, musical trends were growing and changing rapidly. Music of the nineties held something for just about everyone, from the maturing rap and R&B sounds to angst-ridden grunge to bubblegum pop.

■ LYRICS AND BEATS: RAP AND HIP-HOP

Rap music of the late eighties was a politically charged social commentary, calling out hardships for African Americans. Into the nineties, rap increasingly referred to violence and drug use, railed against police, and degraded women. This style was called gangsta rap and earned artists Dr. Dre, Snoop Doggy Dogg, and others criticism for their songs' highly controversial lyrics. A rivalry developed between East Coast rappers, such as Sean "Puffy" Combs and the Notorious B.I.G., and West Coast rappers, such as Dr. Dre, Tupac (2Pac) Shakur, and Snoop Dogg. The murders of 2Pac and the Notorious B.I.G. in 1996 and 1997, respectively, only heightened rap's association with violence. Nonviolent rap from MC Hammer, along with melodic R&B from Boyz II Men, countered those tough performances in the first half of the decade.

Unlike many male groups, female R&B and hip-hop artists scored hits with songs that had positive messages. Queen Latifah, Salt-n-Pepa, TLC, and En Vogue sang about safe sex, avoiding drugs, and treating women with

The rapper, singer, and actress known as Queen Latifah *(right)* was born Dana Owens in Newark, New Jersey, in 1970. At the age of eight, a cousin started calling her "Latifah," meaning "sensitive" in Arabic. The nickname stuck. A gifted student, Latifah started performing in high school and never stopped. In her second year, she formed a rap group with two friends called Ladies Fresh. Latifah was the vocal percussionist, or beatboxer, for the group. Once the group began recording, her mother suggested that she add "Queen" to her name.

After high school, Latifah joined a series of rap groups and performed odd jobs before getting a break in 1988. Fab 5 Freddy, host of *Yo! MTV Raps*, introduced her to the record company that produced her first album, *All Hail the Queen*, in 1989. The album brought her acclaim and the Best New Artist of 1990 Award from the New Music Seminar in Manhattan.

Latifah wanted her songs to counter rap that put women down. Her second single, *Ladies First*, hailed black women for their contributions to black civil rights movements. The rap classic entered the Rock and Roll Hall of Fame as one of 500 Songs That Shaped Rock and Roll.

While Latifah was becoming Queen of Rap, she branched out into other art forms. She acted in television and movies, including Spike Lee's *Jungle Fever* in 1991. She joined the television sitcom *Living Single* for five years. By 1998 Latifah recorded her fourth hip-hop album *Order in the Court* and continued to earn awards for her music and acting into the next century.

respect. Missy Elliott broke onto the scene in 1997 and became a top-selling hip-hop artist with her blunt lyrics.

Though the U.S. hip-hop world was dominated by African Americans, white men occasionally scored rap hits as well. Vanilla Ice's "Ice Ice Baby" of 1990 made him a one-hit wonder, while Eminem's brash lyrics and attitude earned him fame in 1999. The Beastie Boys, pioneers of hip-hop in the eighties, continued their success in the nineties with their unique blend of hip-hop and punk.

■ ALTERNATIVE AND GRUNGE

Alternative rock appealed to musicians and listeners who rejected the commercial pop music and rap that dominated the airwaves. Alternative bands claimed to be antimainstream. Some artists and critics used *alternative* as an umbrella term for "cutting-edge music."

The music most associated with alternative sounds and Generation X was grunge. Grunge offered strong guitar riffs, heavy beats, and lyrics that reflected social concerns. Band members shunned superficial, big-business-dominated pop culture. Performers wore ripped flannel shirts and torn jeans.

Alternative music reached large audiences via MTV and Lollapalooza, the touring festival of alternative groups including Nine Inch Nails and Smashing Pumpkins. But Nirvana's 1991 breakthrough album, *Nevermind*, with the grunge anthem "Smells Like Teen Spirit," proved grunge could also be commercially successful. The album quickly topped the charts and attracted new listeners to grunge music. Pearl Jam followed Nirvana's success with its first album *Ten*. After the shocking 1994 suicide of Nirvana's front man, Kurt Cobain,

Fans in New Jersey rock out at a music performance during the **LOLLAPALOOZA** music festival in 1993. Lollapalooza was created by Jane's Addiction lead singer, Perry Farrell, in 1991 and ran every summer until 1997. It was revived in 2003.

At the 1993 MTV Video Music Awards, the Seattle grunge band **PEARL JAM** took home the Video of the Year award for its smash hit "Jeremy."

remaining band members went separate ways. Pearl Jam and other bands, such as Soundgarden, Smashing Pumpkins, and Stone Temple Pilots, continued to draw crowds. But by the late nineties, the grunge movement had slowed.

In its place, alternative rock continued as the antidote to pop music. Bands such as Bush, Weezer, Green Day, Rage Against the Machine, Beck, Foo Fighters (headed by Nirvana bandmate Dave Grohl), and piano-driven Ben Folds Five scored top-selling records and a huge following. A revival of ska and swing music in the late nineties also launched bands No Doubt, the Mighty Mighty Bosstones, and the Brian Setzer Orchestra to the top of the charts.

◼ GRRRL POWER

Strong female solo artists including Madonna and Janet Jackson had achieved success in the eighties. Going into the 1990s, new female entertainers, such as Mariah Carey, Celine Dion, Jewel, Alanis Morissette, and R&B's Toni Braxton, took center stage. The difference between eighties and nineties female artists was their ability to control what they sang and how they performed.

❝ Alternative rock doesn't seem so alternative anymore. Every major label has a handful of guitar-driven bands in shapeless shirts and threadbare jeans . . . who conceal catchy tunes with noise and hide craftsmanship behind nonchalance.❞

—Jon Pareles, music critic for the New York Times, 1993

Kurt Cobain, the lead singer and songwriter of Nirvana, was a talented and troubled person. After his parents divorced in 1976 when he was nine, Cobain bounced from relative to relative, never feeling at home. He began to experiment with drugs. His one refuge was a guitar his uncle gave him as a teenager.

Cobain credited punk rock with changing his life. In 1986 he left his hometown of Aberdeen, Washington, for Olympia. There he was in a series of bands before forming Nirvana with bass player Krist Novoselic and various drummers (Dave Grohl joined in 1990). Nirvana recorded its first album, *Bleach*, for an independent Seattle label in 1989. Positive reviews led to Nirvana becoming the first alternative band to sign with a major U.S. label. The band released its CD *Nevermind* in 1991 with the lead single "Smells Like Teen Spirit."

Cobain's songs shouted at listeners with passionate, personal lyrics. They struck a chord with disaffected teens. Within a short time, *Nevermind* sold ten million copies and earned the group $550 million. The overnight success shocked the twenty-four-year-old. He worried about losing control of his music and how fans interpreted the songs. He turned to drugs to help him cope.

In 1992 he married Courtney Love, lead singer of the band Hole. Their baby Fran-

KURT COBAIN of Nirvana is one of the iconic musicians of the 1990s.

ces Bean was born shortly thereafter. The following year, Nirvana recorded *In Utero*, featuring songs about Cobain's shaky marriage and personal struggles. His drug habit, health problems, and inability to deal with sudden popularity overwhelmed him, causing severe depression. In April 1994, Cobain was found dead in his Seattle home with a gunshot wound to his head and a suicide note lying nearby. Although headlines proclaimed him "the voice of a generation," friends and devotees pointed out that was exactly what he didn't want to be.

GWEN STEFANI of No Doubt belts out a song during a concert in 1997.

Female alternative artists and bands gave a loud, unapologetic voice to feminism in the Riot Grrrl movement, begun in the early nineties. The underground punk movement grew into a mainstream trend as celebrity Riot Grrrls, such as Courtney Love of the band Hole and No Doubt's Gwen Stefani, rejected traditionally feminine norms. The raw sounds and attitude of the movement sparked new interest among young women in playing rock music. The movement also spawned new fashions. Riot Grrrls everywhere sported piercings, dyed hair, and short skirts or dresses paired with combat boots.

Female artists across all genres addressed bold topics in their songs. "Instead of guys singing about cars and surfing and making it with chicks . . . it was girls singing about menstruation, date rapes, and making it with other girls . . . ," wrote music critic James Dickerson. The industry was also changing in their favor. Picking up on the new girl power, record companies began to look for female artists to market.

Singer-songwriter Sarah McLachlan decided it was time to showcase women musicians. She organized an all-female rock festival called Lilith Fair that included producers as well as performers. On July 5, 1997, Lilith Fair began its six-week, coast-to-coast concert tour rotating more than sixty artists. Critics doubted that an all-women program would sell enough tickets. But Lilith Fair grossed $16 million from thirty-eight shows and another $4 million from a CD of event highlights—twice as much as the male-dominated Lollapalooza. During its second year, Lilith Fair reached fifty-seven U.S. stages and opened in Europe, Australia, and Japan.

Many performers from the eighties who participated in Lilith Fair in the nineties marveled at their younger musical sisters. Singer Pat Benatar commented, "These women were totally empowered. . . . These women are the product of what we did to get through it [rise in the music business]. . . . For them, it is not a question of, 'Do we deserve it, can we have it?' In their mind, it's, 'Yeah, we deserve it,' and 'Yeah, we want to have it.'"

■ LATIN EXPLOSION

Increased numbers of immigrants and new citizens in the nineties boosted interest in Latin beats—and not just among Latinos. Latin music went mainstream, featuring new performers while rediscovering those who had come earlier.

Ricky Martin, Selena, Jennifer Lopez, Enrique Iglesias, and Marc Anthony benefited from being part of the MTV generation. They were young, talented, and attractive—perfect for music video performances. Martin gained fame in Mexico, Puerto Rico, and South America before taking the United States by storm. The other U.S.-born bilingual talents sang, danced, and acted their way to stardom.

■ COUNTRY CROSSES OVER

Nineties country music stood out for moving closer to mainstream popular music. Country artists recorded hits that topped rock billboard charts and played on pop radio stations. Popular crossover female country singers included LeAnn Rimes, the Dixie Chicks, Shania Twain, and Faith Hill. Male artists Garth Brooks, Tim McGraw, and Steve Earle also achieved some crossover success.

RICKY MARTIN shows off his sexy moves. Music from south of the U.S. border became hugely popular in the 1990s.

BRITNEY SPEARS performed at the Billboard Music Awards in 1999.

■ BUBBLEGUM POP

Pop music of the decade revived an old strategy in making hits. Promoters hand-picked individuals to market as a band. Choices depended upon looks, sex appeal, and dance ability, in addition to musical talent. Songs came second to packaging.

By 1990 the boy band New Kids on the Block was already enjoying huge success. The band became so popular that a wave of packaged stars appeared later in the decade, after grunge's heyday had passed. The worldwide popularity of the Backstreet Boys and *NSYNC in 1997 to 1999 proved the formula still worked. Independently formed 98 Degrees also joined the list of boy bands dominating the charts. Solo artists Britney Spears, Christina Aguilera, Jessica Simpson, and Mandy Moore gained fame through the same type of image making that bundled sexy dance steps, revealing outfits, and simple, infectious melodies. Hanson, a group of three teenage brothers, slightly preceded the larger wave of pop with their original song "MMMBop." The bouncy tune reigned on the airwaves in 1997 and earned the brothers a sizable young female fan base.

■ DANCING IN STEP

As hip-hop culture grew more mainstream, fancy acrobatic moves in break dancing did too. But group dancing became the predominant trend of the 1990s. In 1992 Los Del Rio released the Spanish song "Macarena" about a woman from the neighborhood of La Macarena in Seville, Spain. Almost overnight, the song spread from U.S. Latino communities to mainstream America. The group's 1996 video of the song showed dancers performing a routine with repeated arm motions. This dance caught on as a group dance at parties. Following the video's release, fifty thousand people danced the Macarena in New York City's Yankee Stadium.

Beyond the Macarena, Latino entertainers spurred a wider interest in salsa dancing. Classes sprang up in major cities to teach moves to rhythmic Latin songs. Fashions including silk dresses with cowl-necks and slinky Lycra dresses with spaghetti straps developed to show off swaying bodies.

Country music inspired a craze of line dancing, in which a caller directed rows of dancers to move to Western beats. Some choreographed dances, such as the Electric Slide and the Boot Scootin' Boogie, were widely known and could be performed by a large group with no caller. Serious line dancers created an interest in Western attire complete with decorated cowboy boots.

113

A crowd of line dancers at Cardinal Stadium in Louisville, Kentucky, tries to break the record for the world's largest line dance in 1996. They are doing the **MACARENA**.

An in-line skater wows the crowd at the 1999
X GAMES in San Francisco, California.

CHAPTER TEN

PUSHING BOUNDARIES:

SPORTS AND RECREATION OF THE 1990s

A thletes of traditional sports pushed the limits of skill and daring during the 1990s. Some courted danger, while others broke records. The decade proved to be an exciting ride for women, men, girls, and boys in sports.

■ X GAMES

Sports in the 1980s reflected public interest in health and fitness. But into the 1990s, many young people craved more than regular trips to fitness clubs. Some GenXers wanted excitement. A new wave of athletes and exercisers embraced risky feats with mountain bikes, in-line skates, snowboards, bungee cords, and climbing walls.

In summer 1995, the cable television network ESPN (Entertainment and Sports Programming Network) harnessed these skills into the Extreme Games. Athletes competed in what the mainstream public considered extreme sports. The network set rules and ways to measure performance.

ESPN televised the first Extreme Games from Rhode Island and Vermont. The Extreme Games showcased nine events, including street luge (racing downhill on a type of skateboard, lying on one's back), bungee jumping, water sports, eco-challenge (a multiday team adventure race), in-line skating, skysurfing, sport climbing, biking, and skateboarding. In 1996 the network renamed the Olympic-style competition the X Games. At the X Games, athletes pushed themselves to extremes by performing death-defying and gravity-defying stunts. Nearly two hundred thousand people, mainly young men, watched the first competitions.

Each year the X Games attracted wider audiences and drew more contestants. In 1998 ESPN added the Winter X Games from Aspen, Colorado. Sponsors and advertisers targeted twelve- to thirty-four-year-olds with fashion, music, and product tie-ins. As the X Games gained a following, the sports they featured earned respect among mainstream athletes. As evidence, snowboarding became an Olympic sport in 1998, with giant slalom and half-pipe competitions at the Winter Games in Nagano, Japan.

■ THE DREAM TEAM

Up until 1989, the International Basketball Federation banned professional basketball players from competing in the Olympics. Once the rule changed, the United States assembled a team that included the best men from the NBA (National Basketball Association). USA Basketball, the national team, launched its Dream Team of NBA greats at the 1992 Barcelona Olympic Games in Spain. The team included superstars Michael Jordan (Chicago Bulls), Larry Bird (Boston Celtics), Charles Barkley (Philadelphia 76ers), Magic Johnson (Los Angeles Lakers), Patrick Ewing (New York Knicks), Scottie Pippen (Chicago Bulls), and Karl Malone (Utah Jazz).

Members of the 1996 basketball **DREAM TEAM**, which included *(from left to right)* David Robinson, Scottie Pippen, Mitch Richmond, Reggie Miller, Karl Malone, and Shaquille O'Neal, listen to the U.S. national anthem during the medal ceremony at the 1996 Olympic Games in Atlanta, Georgia.

The Dream Team slammed opponents with their incredible athletic ability and strong teamwork. They won by an average of 43 points per game. During the final game, the United States defeated Croatia 117–85 to win the gold. The Dream Team (featuring several returning stars) repeated their success at the 1996 Atlanta Olympics in Georgia, winning eight games without a single loss.

Although Michael Jordan missed the 1996 Olympics, he stood out as the decade's NBA star with his tough defense and ability to score points. Throughout the nineties, he led the Bulls to six NBA championships (1991–1993, 1996–1998). His playing style and positive public image touched fans around the world. After signing contracts to endorse products, including Nike's top-selling "Air Jordan" athletic shoes, Jordan became the most visible sports figure anywhere.

> **"I can accept failure, but I can't accept not trying."**
>
> — *Michael Jordan, basketball star, 1994*

■ WOMEN'S BASKETBALL

In 1972 Congress passed the landmark Title IX law for equal education, requiring colleges and high schools to provide equal opportunities for girls and boys to play sports. Girls' basketball was one of the earliest sports to make inroads into school schedules. But as with other female sports, few talented players found a place for their athletic skills beyond college. Professional women's basketball leagues came and went, so skilled U.S. players often traveled overseas to find teams that would let them earn a living.

In 1996 the Olympics opened to women's basketball. The U.S. Olympic Committee gathered top players for a national team. They didn't lose a single practice game against college and amateur teams. Reporters called the women the Dream Team too. The Olympics was a huge success for the U.S. women's basketball team. The team played eight games before increasingly larger crowds. By the last game, cheering fans waved signs that read, "The REAL Dream Team." The United States won its final game against Brazil to clinch Olympic gold. "This is a great day for women's basketball," said U.S. forward Sheryl Swoopes.

After the Olympics, talk surfaced about another professional women's league. The American Basketball League (ABL) offered skilled women their first shot at earning a decent living from U.S. basketball. However, the NBA soon announced formation of its Women's National Basketball Association (WNBA). NBA support gave WNBA players a chance to attract the few sponsors and television contracts

THE U.S. WOMEN'S BASKETBALL TEAM celebrates after beating Brazil to win the gold medal in the 1996 Olympic Games in Atlanta.

offered to women's sports. The ABL folded in December 1998. The WNBA flourished, absorbing the former ABL players and coaches.

Basketball developed into the leading women's sport. Cable television broadcast college and professional basketball games. Young girls saw players as role models. By 2000, 17 percent more girls played basketball than in 1990, and numbers kept increasing. Colleges and universities competed for top players by offering scholarships, just as they did for male basketball players. The future of women's sports, especially basketball, looked bright.

■ WOMEN'S WORLD CUP

Soccer, the world's most popular sport, had been a hard sell in the United States. But interest started growing at the student level. The Title IX law led to more soccer teams for girls. Yet, their team successes rarely made headlines.

In 1982 the National Collegiate Athletic Association (NCAA), the ruling body for college sports, hosted the first annual women's championship soccer tournament. Three years later, the U.S. Soccer Federation and the Olympic

Committee backed formation of a team for international competition.

In 1996 women's soccer made its grand entrance at the Olympics in Atlanta, Georgia. U.S. sports fans followed their team's progress. The final game between Norway and the United States attracted the biggest crowd for any women's soccer game. The team won the first U.S. Olympic gold for soccer—men's or women's—2–1.

Three years later, the United States hosted the 1999 World Cup tournament with sixteen teams. The thirty-two World Cup games aired in seventy-seven countries. By then the public knew star players, such as the world's leading scorer, Mia Hamm; the queen of shutouts, goalkeeper Briana Scurry; and defender Brandi Chastain. Ninety thousand fans jammed into the Rose Bowl Stadium in Pasadena, California, to see the final match between the United States and China. The score remained tied at 0–0 at the end of the game. Finally, after two scoreless overtime periods, a penalty-kick shootout decided the game. China missed just one of five shots. But Brandi Chastain shot the United States' fifth scoring kick into the goal, clinching the win. Overcome with joy, Chastain fell to her knees, stripped off her jersey, and waved it overhead to thunderous applause. "Momentary insanity, nothing more, nothing less," said Chastain afterward. "I thought 'My God, this is the greatest moment of my life on the soccer field.'"

The World Cup proved the most successful women's sporting event

After kicking the winning penalty shot to beat China in the 1999 World Cup soccer championship, **BRANDI CHASTAIN'S** reaction was captured in this memorable photo.

in history. The popularity of soccer soared. In 1986 the Soccer Industry Council of America had counted 85,173 girls playing soccer on high school teams. By 1998 more than 7 million girls played soccer in an expanding network of elementary and high school clubs and school teams. The formation of a women's national professional soccer league became a real possibility.

■ MARCH TO THE OLYMPICS: ICE HOCKEY AND SOFTBALL

Women's ice hockey and softball also were added to the Olympics in the 1990s. Before the late 1980s, females interested in playing ice hockey joined male teams. But they often braved teasing and other obstacles. Then, in 1987, Canada hosted the first Women's World Invitational tournament. The level of play proved so strong that the International Ice Hockey Federation organized the Women's World Championship in 1990.

In 1998 the International Olympic Committee opened the Olympic Games in Nagano, Japan, to women hockey teams. That year the United States bested Canada to win the gold. Four years later, women's hockey became a permanent Olympic sport. Female hockey stars, including U.S. Olympic captain Cammi Granato and Canada's tough Manon Rheaume, appeared on cereal boxes, in magazine ads, and in television commercials.

Interest in girl's ice hockey skyrocketed. In 1990, 149 U.S. girls' and women's teams existed. Seven years later, the number climbed to 910. For the first time, talented young female ice hockey players knew they had somewhere to take their skills beyond their childhood rink.

CAMMI GRANATO carries the U.S. flag overhead in a victory lap after the U.S. women's hockey team beat Canada for the gold in the 1998 Winter Olympics in Nagano, Japan.

Women's softball got its Olympic start in 1996. In the games, the United States crushed strong teams from China and Australia, both considered favorites. With the help of pitcher Lisa Fernandez and shortstop Dorothy (Dot) Richardson, the U.S. women's team won the gold. The team's success led to formation of the Women's Pro Softball League in 1997 (renamed National Pro Fastpitch in 2002). The league's six teams and gold-medal winners showed a nation of softball-loving girls they could dream of continuing to play their favorite sport.

■ RECORD BREAKERS

The decade saw many other sports landmarks. Established athletes as well as young stars shattered records and achieved notable firsts.

In baseball some of the sport's biggest stars broke long-held records. Cal Ripken Jr., shortstop for the Baltimore Orioles, played more consecutive games than Lou Gehrig's record 2,130 from 1939. Ripken totaled 2,632 games before missing one on September 21, 1998. Oakland Athletics first baseman Mark McGwire broke Roger Maris's 1961 record of 61 home runs in one season, setting the new record at 70. That same season, Chicago Cubs outfielder Sammy Sosa also surpassed the old record by hitting 66 home runs.

Bicycle racing reached a new level of popularity in 1999 after Lance Armstrong won his first Tour de France, the world-famous cycling race through French towns and

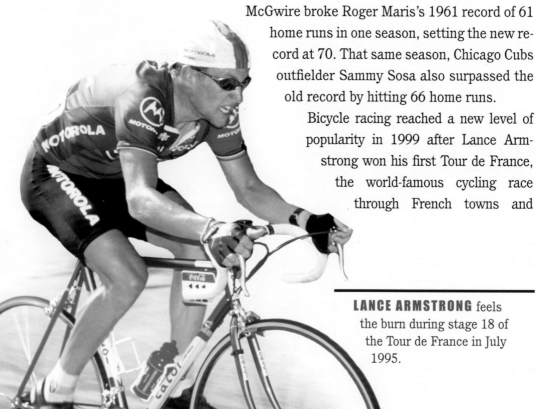

LANCE ARMSTRONG feels the burn during stage 18 of the Tour de France in July 1995.

countryside. Americans rarely won this event, so Armstrong's feat was a victory in itself. But he had recently recovered from life-threatening cancer, for which doctors had given him less than a 50-50 chance to survive. The public had followed his strenuous training after completion of cancer treatment in 1997. They celebrated his resolve to win and prove he could beat the odds. "This is a guy who we saw with no hair, lying in bed barely able to move after brain surgery, and now he's won cycling's greatest race," said Karl Haussmann, director of the Lance Armstrong Cancer Foundation. The Tour de France victory made Armstrong an international hero for his resilience, stamina, and determination. He went on to win the next six Tour de France races as well—a record seven in all.

In tennis, two sisters stole the spotlight and milestone victories. Venus and Serena Williams turned professional as young teens. Venus entered tournaments at the age of fourteen, reaching the U.S. Open final just three years later. At eighteen, she ranked in the top five, propelling serves at 127 miles (204 km) per hour. Serena followed her older sister's lead. Between 1997 and 1999, she went from 304th in world ranking to 21st. In 1999 seventeen-year-old Serena beat Martina Hingis to win the U.S. Open. That year Venus and Serena paired up to win doubles titles at the French Open and U.S. Open, the first sister and African American team to win grand slam doubles titles. They continued to command high rankings and tennis's top prizes into the twenty-first century.

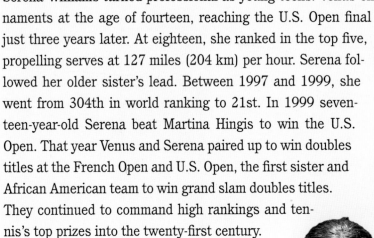

THE WILLIAMS SISTERS, Serena *(left)* and Venus *(right)*, wowed the sports world with their tenacity and powerhouse moves on the court.

Everyone knew that Eldrick "Tiger" Woods *(right)* was a talented boy. He was swinging golf clubs by the age of two and competing in junior tournaments by kindergarten. At fifteen, Woods won his sixth Optimist International Junior tournament and was the youngest player ever to win the U.S. Junior Amateur Championship. In 1994 eighteen-year-old Woods became the youngest-ever U.S. Amateur champion.

Woods left Stanford University to turn professional in 1996. He won his first Professional Golfers' Association of America (PGA) Tour victory at the Las Vegas Invitational. His win over a field of seasoned players quieted doubters who thought him too young to compete—or win. Nike offered Woods an endorsement contract worth $40 million over five years. Titleist, a golf equipment manufacturer, contracted with him for $3 million over three years.

In 1997 Woods won the Masters Tournament with a record score and by a record-breaking twelve strokes. The twenty-one-year-old was the youngest Masters champ and first African American to win a professional golf tournament. By 2000 Woods had won all four major golf championships: the Masters, the U.S. Open, the British Open, and the PGA Championship. He ranked among the top prize winners.

Woods singlehandedly brought golf out of country clubs and to a younger, more diverse crowd. The son of an African American father and Thai mother, he has become the face of golf for a new generation. His successes have continued, but his place as a sports legend was secured long before the end of the nineties.

123

■ POPULAR ACTIVITIES FOR EVERYDAY ATHLETES

Skateboarding had been around for decades, with a resurgence in the 1980s as a "rebel sport." Some communities banned skateboarding in public spaces where it was seen as a nuisance. Once ESPN broadcast the sport in the X Games, however, skateboarding moved closer to mainstream, especially among young people. A few communities built skateboard parks where amateur athletes could practice, keeping skateboarders off city streets.

One recreational trend of the 1990s had more to do with relaxation than activity. Coffee shops became the new default location for meeting with friends or simply refueling on caffeine. During the late 1950s and early 1960s, beatniks had shared poetry in local coffeehouses. But gourmet coffee consumption really became trendy after a little retail coffee shop called Starbucks opened in 1971. Starbucks sold high-end imported fresh-roasted coffee beans and brewing accessories from the Seattle store.

In the 1980s, Howard Schultz, Starbucks' marketing director, introduced the idea of transforming the stores into espresso bars, much like he had seen in Milan, Italy. He suggested making a Starbucks store into a gathering place and serving caffe lattes, mochas, and other coffee drinks. Seattle customers loved the changes. His idea became the model for a national chain of shops that would revolutionize the coffee business.

By 1992 Starbucks had opened 165 outlets across the country. Other individual and chain coffee shops joined the budding coffee craze. In 1994 the sitcom *Friends* debuted and showed its six main characters meeting and hanging out in a coffee shop, further popularizing the idea. From then on, coffee shops have attracted people who wanted their morning jolt as well as those who just preferred a quiet place to meet and hang out.

The in-line skating industry benefited from the X Games too. At one time, mainly ice hockey players bought in-line skates to train off-season. But in the mid-1980s, Rollerblade, Inc., changed the future of in-line skating. The company produced the first comfortable skate with a brake anyone could control. Rollerblade expanded sales to sporting goods stores and increased publicity. Then came the 1995 X Games, showcasing highly skilled "bladers" and exciting tricks. Interest in in-line skates soared. Kids and adults skated in parks and on boardwalks. However, the trend slowed by the end of the decade.

■ RECREATION AT HOME

During the 1990s, popular games and toys ranged from stuffed animals to increasingly advanced gadgets. Families and young adults bought video game systems such as Nintendo, Super Nintendo, Game Boy, Sega, and Sony PlayStation.

Kids check out the new **SUPER NINTENDO ENTERTAINMENT SYSTEM** through a store window in 1991.

While the models of the early nineties had primitive, pixelated graphics, technology improved with each new system and allowed for more advanced games with increasingly realistic images later in the decade. Players spent hours mastering games featuring everything from Super Mario Brothers to car racing to James Bond. Video games became a new staple of home entertainment.

Video game fans found another outlet with the expansion of the Internet. Web-based games allowed people to compete against others around the globe. Advancing graphics and technology paved the way for online role-playing games such as *Lineage* (1998) and *EverQuest* (1999), in which hundreds or even thousands of players could compete in the same fantasy game world. These games surged in popularity early in the next decade, adding to the ways in which the Internet altered human interaction.

For younger kids, the must-have trendy toy of 1996 was less high tech: Tickle Me Elmo. The talking stuffed toy, based on the *Sesame Street* puppet Elmo, laughed hysterically and shook when squeezed. During the holiday season, some shoppers turned violent to beat other customers to a store's limited supply of Elmos. Elmo grew so popular that manufacturers quickly produced Tickle Me Cookie Monster and other dolls from *Sesame Street* characters.

Beanie babies also took the market by storm in 1996, selling out of specialty stores faster than they could be restocked. Each small bean-stuffed plush animal came with a name, birth date, and poem. Beanie babies were originally a children's toy, but they quickly turned into a hot item for collectors of all ages. The craze lasted through 1999.

New Year's Eve revelers ring in the NEW MILLENNIUM in New
York City's Times Square at midnight on January 1, 2000.

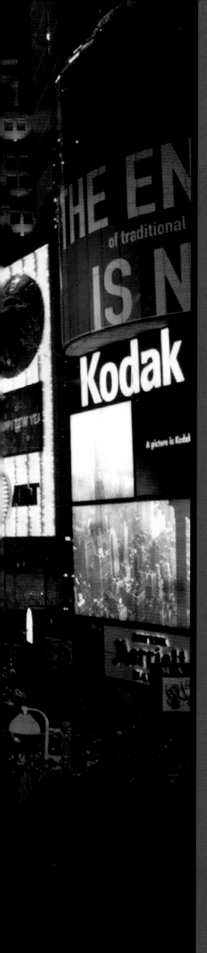

EPILOGUE
THE FAST-CHANGING
WORLD

The 1990s ended with a bang of celebration. The close of 1999 marked the change to a new century as well as a new millennium, and big cities around the globe planned huge parties. From New York to Australia to China, citizens celebrated the close of one century and beginning of another with fireworks, music, and dancing in the streets. Hopes ran high for a productive, peaceful world in the future.

■ Y2K

Despite the cause for celebration, many Americans had anxiety about what would happen when computer clocks switched over to the year 2000, known in techie shorthand as Y2K. To save costs, computer programs had historically been designed with two numbers for the year instead of four (for example, 92 for the year 1992). As 2000 approached, experts realized the two-digit year system would cause computer processors to interpret the change to 00 as reverting back to 1900. Some feared that computers and everything they ran would go haywire at midnight, causing a crisis. Banks would shut down and block access to money. Transportation and distribution systems would stop moving food and supplies across the nation. Missiles and bombs would accidentally fire.

Government and other institutions planned ahead. Many computer companies fixed the glitch, and none of these disasters happened. New Year's entertainment and worldwide celebration went on as intended.

■ 2000 PRESIDENTIAL ELECTION

Though the U.S. economy was strong, the American public had grown tired of the drama of the Clinton administration and battles between political parties in Congress. That made a 2000 presidential bid more difficult for the Democratic nominee, Vice President Al Gore. Republican presidential nominee George W. Bush ran on promises to end bickering between the parties, restore "dignity and honor" to government, and lower federal taxes. Gore criticized Bush's policies as favoring the rich and questioned his record as governor of Texas. He portrayed himself as a leader who would fight for working families.

In the end, the election was one of the closest in history. Gore received slightly more of the popular vote. But in the Electoral College, which decides the election, Florida's twenty-five electoral votes for Bush gave him the lead and won him the election. As local results of Florida's tight race were analyzed, questions swirled about miscounted and uncounted ballots.

The close vote count resulted in a bitter battle requiring ballot recounts.

On November 20, 2000, election officials in Miami-Dade County, Florida, started the manual **RECOUNT OF THE STATE'S VOTES IN THE 2000 PRESIDENTIAL ELECTION**.

This was the first contested U.S. presidential election since 1960 and only the sixth in history. The uncertainty dragged on for more than a month.

U.S. Supreme Court judges finally ruled to stop manual recounts in Florida. With that ruling, the 2000 election became the first presidential race settled in court. Gore ended his challenges to the vote to spare the nation further turmoil, and George W. Bush was sworn in on January 20, 2001. Gore's supporters believed his association with the Clinton administration had cost him the election.

■ CAUSE TO CELEBRATE THE NEW MILLENNIUM

Americans found reason to celebrate the 1990s. The decade was relatively peaceful for the United States. The Cold War had ended, and the United States reduced the number of military and deadly weapons worldwide.

President Clinton left the nation with an economy healthier than the one he had inherited. Government had eliminated the budget deficit. Although the technology bubble showed signs of deflating by late 2000, businesses were strong. Unemployment and inflation reached new lows. Americans from all income levels lived better lives than a decade earlier.

Without constant threats of war, Americans looked for ways to improve their lives and communities. Technology and research had produced miraculous advances. Medical breakthroughs, scientific study, space ventures, and digital communication introduced awesome possibilities. Americans looked forward to what the next century might bring.

DICK CHENEY *(left)* and **GEORGE W. BUSH** *(right)*, with their wives, arrived on the steps of the Lincoln Memorial during the Inaugural opening celebration on January 18, 2001, two days before the inauguration.

1990

- President Bush signs the Clean Air Act to improve air quality.
- Iraq invades Kuwait, prompting the United States to enter the Persian Gulf War.
- The U.S. government funds the Human Genome Project to sequence all the genes in the human body.
- NASA launches the Hubble Space Telescope from the space shuttle *Discovery*.
- The TV sitcom *Seinfeld*, starring comedian Jerry Seinfeld, debuts on NBC.

1991

- President George Bush orders Operation Desert Storm, which pushes Iraqi troops out of Kuwait within one hundred hours.
- Congress confirms Clarence Thomas as a justice on the Supreme Court, despite Professor Anita Hill's damaging public charges of sexual harassment.
- The Soviet Union dissolves and is replaced by independent countries.
- White policemen are videotaped beating African American motorist Rodney King.
- British computer scientist Tim Berners-Lee introduces the World Wide Web.

1992

- A jury acquits the four police who beat Rodney King, triggering race riots in Los Angeles that kill fifty-two people and cost nine hundred thousand dollars in property damage.
- President Bush signs the Americans with Disabilities Act. It ensures equal opportunities in education and training programs for Americans with disabilities.
- Bill Clinton is elected president with Al Gore as his vice president.
- MTV debuts its reality show *The Real World*, featuring seven strangers living together in Brooklyn, New York.
- The Dream Team dominates men's basketball at the 1992 Olympic Games in Barcelona, Spain.

1993

- Lieutenants of a Somali warlord kill eighteen U.S. soldiers after shooting down a U.S. Blackhawk helicopter in Mogadishu. All U.S. troops there are called home.
- President Clinton signs the North America Free Trade Agreement (NAFTA) to boost exchange of business among U.S., Mexican, and Canadian companies.
- A bomb explodes beneath the World Trade Center in New York, killing six people.
- The Branch Davidian cult and FBI exchange gunfire in Waco, Texas, in a battle that results in a fire and the deaths of about eighty cult members.

1994

- Republicans gain control of both houses of Congress, their first sweep in forty years.
- Californians pass Proposition 187, limiting public services for illegal immigrants.
- Kurt Cobain, front man of the grunge band Nirvana, commits suicide.

1995

- O. J. Simpson is arrested on suspicion of murdering his former wife, Nicole, and her friend Ronald Goldman.
- Louis Farrakhan organizes the Million Man March in Washington, D.C.
- Timothy McVeigh bombs the Alfred P. Murrah federal building in Oklahoma City, killing 168 people and injuring 600.
- U.S. troops join NATO peacekeeping forces in Bosnia. Serbian president Slobodan Milosevic signs the Dayton Accord, a treaty to end fighting in Bosnia.
- ESPN organizes and televises the first X Games.

1996

- Bill Clinton wins a second term as president.
- The Unabomber, Ted Kaczynski, is captured at his remote cabin in Montana.
- Madeliene Albright is appointed the first female secretary of state.
- The rock musical *Rent* debuts at the Nederlander Theatre in New York.
- U.S. women sweep Olympic competitions in soccer, basketball, gymnastics, and softball.

1997

- President Clinton meets with world leaders in Kyoto, Japan, to discuss ways to reduce emissions of greenhouse gases.
- Lilith Fair, an all-female concert tour, debuts and earns $16 million.
- Tiger Woods is the first African American to win the Masters Golf Tournament.
- Sitcom star Ellen DeGeneres announces she is a lesbian, two weeks before her character on the show *Ellen* comes out in a highly anticipated episode.

1998

- The film *Titanic* is released in theaters.
- President Clinton helps negotiate a peace agreement between opposing groups in Northern Ireland. Leaders pass the Good Friday Accord.
- U.S. embassies are bombed in Nairobi, Kenya, and Dar es Salaam, Tanzania. The bombings kill 258 people, including 12 Americans, and injure more than 5,000.
- President Clinton's affair with White House intern Monica Lewinsky is reported and investigated. Clinton is impeached but not removed from office.
- Dr. Jack Kevorkian is sentenced to prison for participating in physician-assisted suicides of terminally ill patients.

1999

- Two Columbine High School students shoot to death twelve classmates, one teacher, and themselves in Littleton, Colorado.
- The Dow Jones Industrial Average reaches 11,000 for the first time in history.
- Serena and Venus Williams win doubles tennis titles at the French Open and U.S. Open.

131

5   Editors of Time-Life Books, *The Digital Decade–the 90s* (Richmond, VA: Time-Life Books, 2000), 6.

8   Texas A&M University, "Public Papers: Inaugural Address 1989-01-20," *George Bush Presidential Library and Museum*, January 20, 1989, http://bushlibrary.tamu.edu/research/public_papers.php?id=1&year=&month= (April 10, 2009).

9   George Bush, *All the Best George Bush: My Life in Letters and Other Writings* (New York: Simon & Schuster, 1999), 411.

11–12   George H. W. Bush, quoted in "What's Your Beef?" transcript, *PBS, The NewsHour with Jim Lehrer*, January 20, 1998, 1990–2009, http://www.pbs.org/newshour/bb/law/jan-june98/fooddef_1-20.html (April 16, 2009).

13   George Bush, *All the Best George Bush*, 483.

15   Peter Jennings, *The Century* (New York: Doubleday, 1998), 537.

16   George Tindall and David Shi, *America: A Narrative History*, vol. 2 (New York: W. W. Norton, 2004), 1,192.

16   Ibid., 1,194.

16   Arthur Schlesinger Jr., ed., *The Almanac of American History* (Greenwich, CT: Brompton Books, 1993), 645.

17   Nigel Hamilton, *Bill Clinton: An American Journey* (New York: Random House, 2003), 689.

17   Gwen Ifill, "The 1992 Campaign: New York; Clinton Admits Experiment with Marijuana in 1960s," *New York Times*, March 30, 1992.

18   Hamilton, 681.

18   Bush, 555.

18   Bill Clinton, *My Life* (New York: Alfred A. Knopf, 2004), 490.

19   John T. Woolley and Gerhard Peters, "William J. Clinton," *The American Presidency Project*, http://www.presidency.ucsb.edu/ws/?pid=46366 (April 16, 2009).

19   Bush, 555.

20   Corporation for National and Community Service, "National Service Timeline," *AmeriCorps*, 2009, http://www.americorp.gov/about/ac/history_timeline.asp (April 16, 2009).

21   Barry Goldwater, "Ban on Gays Is Senseless Attempt to Stall the Inevitable," *Washington Post*, June 10, 1993, A23.

21   Clinton, 490.

22   Jonathan Alter, "The Clinton Battle Plan," *Newsweek*, November 27, 2006, 26.

23   Joyce Milton, *The First Partner: Hillary Rodham Clinton* (New York: William Morrow and Company, 1999), 274.

25   Ronald Kessler, *The Bureau: The Secret History of the FBI* (New York: Macmillan, 2003), 374.

25   Tindall and Shi, 1,222.

23   *New York Times*, "Topics of The Times: The Annals of Dessert," September 29, 1993, http://www.nytimes.com/1993/09/29/opinion/topics-of-the-times-the-annals-of-dessert.html (April 16, 2009).

27   Alter, 28.

28   Lance Morrow, "Newt's World," *Time*, December 25, 1995, http://www.time.com/magazine/article/0,9171,983876-1,00.html (April 16, 2009).

28   Robert Reich, *Reason: Why Liberals Will Win the Battle for America* (New York: Knopf, 2004), 39–40.

34   *New York Times*, "Albright, in a Barnard Address, Sees a Trend to U.S. Isolationism," May 17, 1995.

34   Clinton, 858.

36   Ibid., 593.

38   BBC, "BBC on This Day 1993: World Trade Center Bomb Terrorizes New York," *BBC News*, 2008, http://news.bbc.co.uk/onthisday/hi/dates/stories/february/26/newsid_2516000/2516469.stm (April 16, 2009).

40   Clive Irving, ed., *In Their Name* (New York: Random House, 1995), in Stuart Kallen, ed., *The 1990s* (San Diego: Greenhaven Press, 2000), 71.

41 Kenneth T. Walsh, Gloria Borger, Gareth G. Cook and David Hage, "The Price of Victory," *U. S. News & World Report*, August 8, 1993, http://www.usnews.com/usnews/news/articles/930816/archive_015624.htm (April 16, 2009).

45 Microsoft, "Bill Gates: Chairman, Microsoft Corporation," *Microsoft*, 2007, http://www.microsoft.com/PRESSPASS/EXEC/BILLG/BIO.MSPX (April 16, 2009).

46 Jennings, 557.

50 Jennings, 556–557.

53 Nicholas Wade, "New Rules on Use of Human Embryos in Cell Research," *New York Times*, August 24, 2000.

57 Thomas Friedman, *The World Is Flat* (New York: Farrar, Strauss and Giroux, 2005), 293.

60 Clinton, 432.

60 Tindall and Shi, 1,218.

61 Bill Gates, quoted on Association of School and College Leaders, "Leader Magazine: Ctl-Alt-Del," *Leader,* 2009, http://www.leadermagazine.co.uk/article.php?id=738 (June 4, 2009).

63 Danielle Whelton, "Clinton Announces Larger-Than-Expected Surplus," *CNN.com*, October 27, 1999, http://www.cnn.com/ALLPOLITICS/stories/1999/10/27/clinton.surplus/index.html (October 27, 2008).

68 Rachel Swarns, "So Far Obama Can't Take Black Vote for Granted," *New York Times*, February 2, 2007, A17.

69 Tindall and Shi, 1,207–1,208.

71 Mike Wallace, *Between You and Me* (New York: Hyperion, 2005), 209.

71 Ibid., 220.

73 Jennings, 538.

73 Ibid., 542.

73 Ibid., 544.

75 CNN, "CNN–Quotes from the Crowd," *CNN*, October 16, 1995, http://www.cnn.com/US/9510/megamarch/quotes.html (April 16, 2009).

75 Jennings, 548.

75 Ibid.

80 Sana Siwolop, "Guessing the Next Chapter of Virtual Bookselling," *New York Times*, May 14, 1997, http://www.nytimes.com/1997/05/04/business/guessing-the-next-chapter-of-virtual-bookselling.html (March 10, 2009).

82 Karen Karbo, "And Baby Makes Two," *New York Times*, June 27, 1993, http://www.nytimes.com/books/98/10/18/specials/kingsolver-pigs1.html (April 16, 2009).

84 R. L. Stine, "R.L. Stine Bio.," *R. L. Stine Official Website*, 2009, http://www.rlstine.com/#nav/rlstine (April 16, 2009).

91 Suzy Menkes, "RUNWAYS: Fetish or Fashion?" *New York Times*, November 21, 1993, http://www.nytimes.com/1993/11/21/style/runways-fetish-or-fashion.html (April 16, 2009).

94 Harpo Productions, "Oprah's Cut with Martha Stewart," *Oprah.com*, 2009, http://www.oprah.com/article/omagazine/oprahscut/omag_200008_martha (April 16, 2009).

98 Jennings, 532.

98 Eric Levin, ed., *People Yearbook 1998*, (New York: Time Inc. Home Entertainment, 1998), 77.

102 Justine Elias, "James Cameron: The Taskmaster of 'The Titanic,'" *New York Times*, December 14, 1997, http://www.nytimes.com/packages/html/movies/bestpictures/titanic-ar.html?scp=4&sq=james%20cameron%20titanic&st=cse (April 16, 2009).

108 Jon Pareles, "POP VIEW: Great Riffs. Big Bucks. New Hopes?" *New York Times*, February 28, 1993, http://www.nytimes.com/1993/02/28/arts/pop-view-great-riffs-big-bucks-new-hopes.html (September 1, 2007).

110 Editors of Time-Life Books, 127.

111 Ibid., 15.

117 Michael Jordan Quotes/Air Jordan Legacy, "Michael Jordan Quotes," *airjordanlegacy.com*, n.d., http://www.airjordanlegacy.com/michael-jordan-quotes (April 16, 2009).

117 Marlene Targ Brill, *Winning Women in Basketball* (Hauppauge, NY: Barron's, 2000), 16.

119 Lissa Smith, ed., *Nike Is a Goddess* (New York: Atlantic Monthly Press, 1998), 264.

122 CNN/SI, "Austin Power: Armstrong's Victory Inspires Fans Back Home," *CNNSI.com*, July 26, 1999, http://sportsillustrated.cnn.com/cycling/1999/tour_de_france/news/1999/07/25/austin_fans (November 21, 2008).

123 Kathie Fry, ed., "Skateboarding History," *SkateLog.com*, n.d., http://www.skatelog.com/skateboarding/skateboarding-history.htm (October 29, 2008).

128 Alison Mitchell, "The 2000 Campaign: The Strategy; Shifting Tactics, Bush Uses Issues to Confront Gore," *New York Times*, September 16, 2000, http://www.nytimes.com/2000/09/16/us/2000-campaign-strategy-shifting-tactics-bush-uses-issues-confront-gore.html (May 27, 2009).

SELECTED BIBLIOGRAPHY

Anderson, Annelise, ed. *Thinking about America: The United States in the 1990s*. Lanham, MD: Hoover Press Publication, 1998.
This collection of essays written by conservatives for the Hoover Institution at Stanford University offers a perspective on urban living, social issues, and economy.

Bush, George. *All the Best George Bush: My Life in Letters and Other Writings*. New York: Simon & Schuster, 1999.
After he left office, President George H. W. Bush compiled his key documents into a book. This text is valuable in exploring the actions and motives behind his responses to key moments in history.

Clinton, Bill. *My Life*. New York: Alfred A. Knopf, 2004.
The lengthy volume tells the story of a critical political figure of the 1990s, President Bill Clinton, in his own words.

Felder, Deborah. *A Century of Women*. Secaucus, NJ: Carol Publishing Group, 1999.
This review of women's struggles and achievements during the last century highlights women of the nineties and what they accomplished.

Friedman, Thomas. *The World Is Flat*. New York: Farrar, Straus and Giroux, 2005.
This journalist and observer of politics and the economy offers a world perspective on the U.S. economy and forces that drive it.

Hamilton, Nigel. *Bill Clinton: An American Journey*. New York: Random House, 2003.
This biography of the forty-second president offers an insider's perspective of what drives the life and politics of the man.

Kallen, Stuart, ed. *The 1990s*. San Diego: Greenhaven Press, 2000.
The essay collection covers the history, politics, and current events of the 1990s written by experts in their particular fields.

Levin, Eric, ed. *People Yearbook 1998*. New York: Time Inc. Home Entertainment, 1998.
The biography collection points out icons of the nineties and clarifies why they attracted so much attention.

Schlesinger, Arthur, Jr., ed. *The Almanac of American History*. Greenwich, CT: Brompton Books, 1993.
This year-by-year account features social, political, and biographical highlights of the 1990s.

Smith, Lissa, ed. *Nike Is a Goddess*. New York: Atlantic Monthly Press, 1998.
This thorough history of women in sports covers the rise of women in traditional and nontraditional sports as well as battles fought by current well-known athletes to be allowed to play at all.

Tindall, George, and David Shi. *America: A Narrative History*. Vol. 2. New York: W. W. Norton, 2004. These two historians present a unique perspective on the last decade of the twentieth century. They cover foreign and domestic policies and how presidents Bush and Clinton differed on social and political issues of the time.

Wallace, Mike. *Between You and Me*. New York: Hyperion, 2005. The host of the news magazine *60 Minutes* has interviewed key figures in U.S. history. His collection of favorite interviews includes many from the 1990s. This book gives voice to those who were involved in shaping the nineties.

TO LEARN MORE

Books

Aaseng, Nathan. *The Impeachment of Bill Clinton*. San Diego: Lucent Books, 2000. President Clinton had one of the nation's most controversial presidencies. The book explores his journey from Hope, Arkansas, to his White House days and the issues that shaped his time in office.

Dickerson, James. *Go, Girl, Go! The Women's Revolution in Music*. New York: Schirmer Trade Books, 2005. This review of American women in popular music offers a glimpse of the battles females faced and the successes they won on their climb to the top of rock music charts.

Jennings, Peter, and Todd Brewster. *The Century for Young People*. New York: Doubleday, 1999. This overview of the twentieth century hits highlights of the century, focusing on politics, trends, and social movements. The text is an adapted version of an adult book with the same name and by the same noted journalists.

Kallen, Stuart. *The History of Rock and Roll*. Farmington Hills, MI: Lucent Books, 2003. Rock and roll did not appear one day in the fifties. The musical form developed for decades from a long line of musical traditions and continues to evolve. This text follows the journey of this popular form of music.

Kerns, Ann. *Martha Stewart*. Minneapolis: Twenty-First Century Books, 2007. This self-made businesswoman was an important figure in the 1990s. Read about her various career ventures, from television personality to business entrepreneur.

Márquez, Herón. *Latin Sensations*. Minneapolis: Twenty-First Century Books, 2001. Singers Jennifer Lopez, Ricky Martin, Marc Anthony, Enrique Iglesias, and Selena brought Latin music to the mainstream U.S. music scene during the 1990s. This book profiles each star's rise to fame and explores the influence of Latin music's new global popularity.

McPherson, Stephanie Sammartino. *Tim Berners-Lee: Inventor of the World Wide Web*. Minneapolis: Twenty-First Century Books, 2010.
This biography chronicles the life of Tim Berners-Lee and his development of the World Wide Web.

Parker, Steve. *1990s Electronic Media*. Milwaukee: Gareth Stevens, 2002.
Technology played an enormous role in the economy and advances that took place in the nineties. This book covers new and adapted forms of electronic media.

Roberts, Jeremy. *Tiger Woods: Golf's Master*. Minneapolis: Twenty-First Century Books, 2009.
Tiger Woods rose to international fame in the 1990s. Learn more about his life in this engaging biography.

Shields, Charles. *The 1993 World Trade Center Bombing*. New York: Chelsea House, 2002.
The first bombing of the World Trade Center shattered illusions that the United States was immune to terrorist attack on home ground. This book covers this fateful attack, offering events leading up to it and discussing the aftermath.

Films

The Big One. DVD. Los Angeles: Miramax Home Entertainment, 1998.
Michael Moore directed this biting documentary about corporate greed. In the movie, he criticizes mass layoffs in major industries despite record profits. He targets the record industry but also singles out companies, such as Nike, for leading the trend to outsource production to foreign countries that pay workers less than in the United States.

Bill Clinton: Hope, Charisma, and Controversy. DVD. New York: A&E Home Entertainment, 2005.
This video traces Clinton's life from his high school days to the White House.

Bill Gates: Sultan of Software. DVD. New York: A&E Television Network, 2004.
This video tells the story of how a college dropout founded a software business and became one of the world's wealthiest people.

Websites

American Cultural History–Decade 1991–1999
http://kclibrary.nhmccd.edu/decade90
This site identifies highlights of the 1990s. Sections break down politics, fashion, literature, music, and other cultural indicators of the decade.

Hubble's Eye on the Cosmos
http://hubblesite.org/hubble_discoveries
Sending the Hubble into orbit was a major advance in space technology. This site defines and documents the technology and shows how a Hubble model is made.

The 1990s Fashion History
http://www.fashion-era.com
This site offers a bird's-eye view of fashion in the 1990s. It covers trends and illustrates the decade's highlights and low points in fashion.

R.L. Stine's Life Story
http://www.rlstine.com
Who can tell about an author's life better than the author? This site features the life and accomplishments of a beloved children's book author who made reading about ghosts and horror fun for young audiences.

USA Basketball: Men's Olympic History
http:www.usabasketball.com/history
Besides baseball, basketball is one of the United States' most popular team sports. This site tells how the U.S. invention became a world-class Olympic sport.

SELECTED 1990s CLASSICS

Books

Frazier, Charles. *Cold Mountain*. New York: Atlantic Monthly Press, 1997.
Frazier's award-winning historical-fiction adult novel won the 1997 National Book Award. It tells of a wounded Civil War soldier who abandons the Confederate army to return to his love and North Carolina home. The book sold millions and was turned into a film that received seven Academy Award nominations.

Rowling, J. K. *Harry Potter and the Sorcerer's Stone*. New York: Scholastic, 1998.
This young-adult title is the first in the world-captivating seven-book series. The series features a young wizard orphan, his encounters with evil, and his adventures in wizard school.

Sachar, Louis. *Holes*. New York: Scholastic, 1998.
This quirky story follows a supposedly bad boy to reform camp. Those who run the camp believe that redemption comes from digging holes in the hot desert, although they have secret reasons for this form of punishment. The book earned the 1999 Newbery Medal and became a movie in 2002.

Films

Jurassic Park. DVD. Burbank, CA: Warner Bros., 1993.
Steven Spielberg created this science fiction blockbuster from Michael Crichton's novel and screenplay about genetically altered dinosaurs that run amuck in an amusement park. The visually stunning, action-packed film generated nationwide dinomania and was followed by two sequels.

A League of Their Own. DVD. Culver City, CA: Sony Pictures, 1992.
Director Penny Marshall made this groundbreaking movie about an American women's baseball league that gained fame during World War II in the 1940s. The movie featured a star-studded cast, including Tom Hanks as the boozy team manager and Geena Davis, Rosie O'Donnell, and Madonna as athletic teammates.

Titanic. DVD. Los Angeles: Paramount, 1999.
The epic love story that unfolds between Rose (Kate Winslet) and Jack (Leonardo DiCaprio) aboard the doomed 1912 ocean liner captivated audiences in 1997. Larger-than-life visuals and a tragic reenactment of the sinking ship made the movie as monumental as its namesake. The film shattered box office records and earned eleven Academy Awards, including Best Picture and best director for James Cameron.

1990s ACTIVITY

Identify six to ten things in your own life or family history that relate to the 1990s. (To start your thinking, consider events in your family's life, family collections, your house or buildings in your neighborhood, favorite movies, books, songs, and places you've visited.) Use photographs, mementos, and words to create a print or computer scrapbook of your 1990s connections.

INDEX

140

141

144